The Dao of Doug:

The Art of Driving a Bus
OR Finding Zen in San
Francisco Transit: A Bus
Driver's Perspective

DOUGLAS MERIWETHER

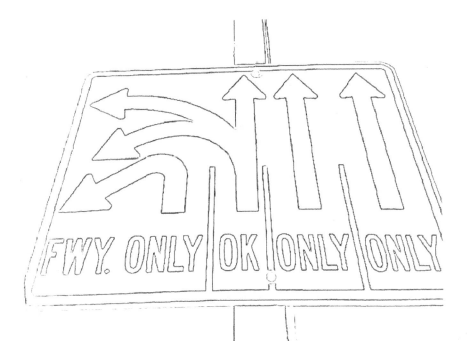

The Dao of Doug:

The Art of Driving a Bus OR Finding Zen in San Francisco Transit: A Bus Driver's Perspective

BALBOA.
PRESS

A DIVISION OF HAY HOUSE

Balboa Press books may be ordered through booksellers or by contacting:

Balboa Press
A Division of Hay House
1663 Liberty Drive
Bloomington, IN 47403
www.balboapress.com
1 (877) 407-4847

Print information available on the last page.

ISBN: 978-1-4525-6649-8 (sc)
ISBN: 978-1-4525-6651-1 (hc)
ISBN: 978-1-4525-6650-4 (e)

Library of Congress Control Number: 2013900153

Balboa Press rev. date: 09/21/2016

"The Dao of things cannot be complete without the Dao of Driving a bus. I'd ride with Doug all the way to the Himalayas just to listen to the art of his wisdom."
David Biddle, author of "Implosions of America--A Story Collection"

"Nice read. I like the mix of situational context and life lessons."
Chad Upham, graduate, Art Center College of Design

"Back Door!" Brandon Stanton

for: my leader and my follower

thanks to :
Ann Delay, Steven Whitworth, and Cyndia Chambers
for help with the title of this book

"Any Life worth living is worth writing about"
-- Anthony Robbins

Contents

Foreword

THIS IS THE NINTH EDITION to Finding Zen in San Francisco. If you'd like this most current version, it is an automatic upload when you click on to the e-reader version online. You must, however, type in 'softcover new' if buying outside of the Balboa Press website. If you see me in person, I always carry a couple of copies with me at all times. All format versions are available at www.daoofdoug.com. By the fall of 2016, this website will have two way email communication so you can give feedback or hear from me directly. And hear from you I do! Everyone has a story to tell me about Muni and questions about why buses are late, passing up, or non-existent.

I have struggled with self-sufficiency and independence all my life by blazing ahead without asking for help from others, and writing this book was no exception. Like the adage about the heroic mail carrier, I have always thought that keeping the bus moving through rain, sleet, and dead of night was the path to success. This, however, is seldom possible in downtown San Francisco on Market Street during rush hour! Keeping to the schedule has not led to any such success that I can see.

The editing, marketing, and production of the book was an area out of my expertise, and I had to learn about these aspects of publishing with professional help. Rather than go to writing workshops or groups, I pushed ahead alone. Removing typos and word crimes from earlier editions could have been avoided with a professional edit. Having the time to interview or get the word out would have also helped! Working full time on the bus and managing this project has been interesting to say the least. The feelings of being a failure or a success can turn on a dime at any street corner or bus stop.

Knowing and meeting Muni at the door is not an attempt at the disunity of superiority. Fellow operators who tell a new hire that "I know everything" when I hand them my book means I have largely failed in my endeavor in writing this book. I laughed really hard at a reviewer that stated "tourists will be disappointed" in reading this book. Perhaps, but not as disappointing as trying to board and ask questions about where I go or what I do when I am late and full. Or freezing in the cold foggy wind in shorts without a jacket. State where you need to go with the cross street or pinpoint the name of a major destination. Our bus shelters display a great transit map with all the details of routes, frequency, and hours of operation.

Offering a copy of this book to an angry passenger brought me to a hearing with charges of unsafe behavior. But an angel was onboard at the time and filled out a courtesy card discounting everything on the complaint against me. This dovetails nicely with the last chapter When Worlds Collide. A passenger had my back. Emotional availability is lacking when an argument arises, so the key is to be spiritually fit and aware and spot trouble before it happens. Thus the term Dao, which means a manner or way of living. If I can keep my way attuned to what I have been taught and understand why the rules are here to protect me, I am on the right path.

Five new chapters have been added, and repetitious content has been reduced. I am trying to keep interest past the first 20 pages. Changes of bus line numbers such as the 71L becoming the 7R and 14R for 14L, for example, have been updated since the first printing in January of 2013. I noticed one pattern writers have without an edit; they repeat themselves, and also fail to make paragraph breaks within standard. My hope is that you pick this book back up after you put it down. Making time to read for most of us has become increasingly difficult in this electronic era of 'convenience'.

Thanks for riding!   Thanks for reading!   Driver Doug   6.26.16

Preface

THIS BOOK WAS MEANT TO be read in short doses, such as a chapter a day, like in a meditation book. This explains why some common points come up in more than one chapter, and repeat. This was intentional. These chapters are more like a weekly blog on a social media website, and were posted as such to be like a topic of the day. So why did I write this book? If I learned anything from my grade school speech teacher, or my university creative writing professor, one of the first ups is: Who is your audience? I would say I have several groups of people in mind for this book. First, students in the training division who have recently applied for a job as a transit operator. Second, those considering a job for the city. And third, passengers who have wondered what we go through, or how do we handle doing such a job.

Then there are the tourists visiting our city who might want reading material on the flight to SFO, or perhaps my friends who grew up with me and wonder just what the heck my life is like here in San Francisco. And then the other more passive audience are those who still own cars, or drive most places to get around. It is my hope if I can get one more car off of the street because of this book, then I can feel like I am doing some good in getting this word out.

I enjoy the fact I don't have a car. But I sure would love a Tesla. Or the new Ford Focus that gets 40 miles per. But just because I am happy our cars are becoming more efficient, it doesn't mean I am going to lease or own one. The last group I have written this book for is for those who have cars and haven't considered taking mass transit. I get people on my bus who have cars in the shop who try transit for the first time.

Taking my car to the shop was just another straw that broke my camel's back in convincing me there had to be a better way to life. And this is what I have found here in this dense city. True, the cost of rent is high, but so are wages. By dumping the car, I found a higher standard of living than the supposed convenience of the suburbs and drive thru culture. A meal at an Olive Garden may be cheap compared to Squat and Gobble here in the city, but at what cost does this Olive Garden meal imply?

I don't trust our representatives to make the changes in transport we so desperately need because they are driving around looking for parking also. Most of my coworkers drive cars and they don't want to pay for parking either. But the notion parking should be free is killing this city and other cities on the West Coast. The traffic on I-5 from San Diego to Seattle is just awful. I don't know when the tipping point will be reached, but it is coming. And I hope this book helps.

I don't have a car so I don't pay for parking. I don't pay for gas, new car battery, jumper cables, car insurance, deductibles, oil, brakes, or checkups. I have two bikes and the repair bill rarely goes over 150 dollars. For 150 dollars I get all new brakes and cables. And these last for over two years. I just don't see that in owning or caring for a car. I walk or ride to work, and my bus is all electric. The electricity comes from hydroelectric power, so no carbon emissions result. This is clean living. I am trying to breathe deep and appreciate the fresh air after a rain storm. Hopefully, this book is a breath of fresh air. Thanks for riding an electric bus!

Doug Meriwether,
San Francisco
November 5, 2012

I'd Never Do Your Job

I COME FROM A BACKGROUND where money may not be the root of all evil, and it was acknowledged that it did indeed grow on trees, but that there were two types of money: Good money and bad money. You never wanted to throw good money after bad. And there was a nuance between money earned and money given. Or money found by luck, or money made easy. I never heard too much about money made easy. Honest money made was the best money. A penny saved was a penny earned. But, boy did that sound like a lot of plodding and not too much fun. So it should come as no surprise, if I worked hard to make money, it should therefore be good money. I was pleased to find work as a transit operator in the city by the bay, the Bagdad by the bay, the city that never sleeps, which was a hard job but a good paying job. I hit the family ancestral jackpot. I was making good money at a hard job in line with my family history.

But I noticed early on in my Muni riding days, that some drivers looked relatively relaxed, and nothing seemed to phase them. And some were actually fun to talk to. And that there did seem to be a way in which to make their work look easy and relaxing, and yet is a high paying job. So the seed was planted early on that this might be a good job for me. As a Gemini sun sign, transportation and continual movement fits my sign.

My 4th grade art project was a drawing of the silver GM coaches that serviced the NY Port Authority from Jersey during the 60's. Bus Driver is a job I have desired since the fourth grade. I have heard those who are successful in their jobs later in life, had a passion for those activities or skills from an early age.

But unlike Civil Engineer, Medical Doctor, Dentist, or Lawyer, Bus Driver did not seem to appear on the success roster. But I didn't really care. Ralph Kramden was my hero. I saw no matter how half baked an idea was that I could hatch, as long as I had my friends, and made a connection with others, everything would turn out okay. When Jackie Gleason would exclaim, "How Sweet it Is!" I got it. I guess you could say that in a way, "The Honeymooners" was my imprint version of "The Wonder Years," many followed in their youth in the eighties.

Fast forward to San Francisco and the late nineties. Newly elected Mayor Willie L. Brown Jr., Esq., was mandated to fix Muni in his first 100 days, and he took immediate action to hire more bus drivers. I went to the Moscone job fair and put into get on the list. Finally, at age 39, I was making a plan about choosing a job that seemed more like a career or occupation than just a need to get another paycheck fast. I encourage anyone living paycheck to paycheck, or between jobs, to pause and look deep about what kind of service they want to provide to others. I would sit near the front seat when I rode the bus with Grandma. I liked it when the bus driver would talk to me. I still do, conditions permitting, and I feel like I am actually in a recruitment mode. Early first impressions can and do have a lasting effect on our life decisions later on down the road. Get them when they are young, and so I present myself as doing a fun job.

The first thing that comes up about why someone would not want my job is, "the people." But where in the world do we not have a job involving other people? And if I am to be resentment free, can I not take quiet time every day to see what amends I can make to determine my part in any negative reaction? To me this is where the rubber meets the road. The path that separates the men from the boys. I see so many miserably quiet lives departing the bus after work daily I sometimes feel like I am the only happy bozo on the bus! Gee, is it that bad? And if I smile, I try to break the grimace of the boarding face. Usually it works.

I guess I need to do more research about why someone would never do my job, but I guess in a way it adds to my job security. Most people don't realize once the mental hurdles are pushed into the background, it is the physical stress that can take its toll and put continued work into jeopardy. Stopping and starting, braking on a downhill with a full load: day in and day out. As Harrison Ford quipped in one of his action movies after incredible odds, "It's not the years, it's the mileage."

When my body starts to give me pain in a certain area, I take care of it immediately! I take care of the warning signs before I can barely step off the bus at the terminal because my hams and quads are all locked up. Repetitive stress requires repetitive stretching and massage.

Just as I have learned to eat on the fly, or pick food choices which are simple to munch on with only a few minutes of recovery time, so too, must we stretch and find a trainer or massage therapist we can meet on a regular basis to prevent our bodies from shutting down. I find myself going to Yoga on a regular basis. Going on leave is not the answer. Shutting down and doing nothing is never a good idea. So as long as we keep moving, we stay employed and enjoy the benefits of steady pay.

I envy musicians and artists who can bring home the bacon with their creative abilities, but also do other part time jobs to stay busy. There can be freedom in scheduling a week with personal choices rather than the ball and chain of a railway timetable, but I guess each lifestyle has it ups and its downs. There are those of us with stable government jobs who would do well to understand the creative mix of those who rotate with three part time jobs and free lance, to make ends meet. The lack of understanding about what needs be done to be work flexible, might lower tensions among the classes of workers who board the bus. Getting to the Zen zone keeps this in balance. I certainly have had to deal with these demons at the fare box, or when someone is running to get to the door.

Yard-starter

WHEN WE START OUR DAY, we pass by the receiver, sign in for our coach, and then see the yard-starter if we have no coach assigned to us. The receiver has our bundle, called a paddle, which includes our run's timetable with scheduled checkpoints, books of transfers, defect card, and any bulletins we need be aware of such as permanent or temporary bus stop changes, construction alerts, lane or street detours, or battery power re-routes.

These are important jobs at Muni. The job duties require personality management, if such a thing is possible. The receiver and yard-starter must juggle several balls without dropping them, and can get pressure from any one of a number of sources: the operator, the shop, dispatch, or central control, just to name a few. And all of this bombardment comes with getting a bus into revenue service, on time and without incident. As a driver, I have the benefit of being captain of the ship, so to speak, and rarely have contact with my coworkers while in the cockpit, moving down the street. The only time we get to see each other is when we get a coach in the morning, or when we pull-in.

Sometimes we need to go to another barn on the weekend and operate a motor-coach as a shuttle around a special event such as a street fair, parade, or demonstration. San Francisco must be number one in street events and reroutes. If there is anything that belies *The city that knows how*, it is transit flexibility to make changes to a line that will engage extra crowds and capacity. We plan our day based upon where we start and finish, and how long it will take to get home from a relief point. It makes for never a dull moment and its why I love being a bus driver in San Francisco.

Construction re-routes and detours are currently high on the list for choice of equipment. With sewer and water line reconstruction we may need diesel buses because the wires are turned off, or we have to maneuver in to opposite lanes where our poles won't reach. The 49 line has been moved to a motor-coach division due to major construction on Van Ness Avenue. This dig will continue for several years and reduce traffic to a single lane in each direction.

The receiver has our paddles laid out on a table in what is called the receiver's area, and if our paddle is missing, it means we have to see the dispatcher for mail about a status upgrade in our training or medical card. If we need a day off or a change in an upcoming schedule, we also see the dispatcher to fill out one of several forms to modify our detail. The dispatcher's office is generally not the place to be a victim or crybaby. Get in, get out, and wait for the words, "I'll pay you for time." or "You're on the sick book." or "You got your one day vacation." *Yes.* And be gone.

If my paddle is missing in the receiver's office, it is because I have mail. These *love letters* contain a nice laundry list of rules violations that we must atone for in a conference or hearing to be assigned a penalty such as unpaid time off. With this comes the decision to open the letter when signing for it, or to wait until after the day is over. I prefer to open my mail after my day is over. I appreciate the mercy of Central Control calling me to see the dispatcher near the end of my day and not the first thing! Sometimes I conveniently forget that they called and I have mail waiting. The tone of voice of the receiver in the morning, or of central control over the air can sometimes be telling, or it can be confounding. When I don't have a clue about what it could be, I can't stand the suspense. I have to open the letter some time later in the day. Ouch. Whoops. Really?

The receivers' area, on the other hand, is where the latest really bad joke can be told, or retold, or modified, or extended, or made into a complete lie. The art, of course, being in how realistic the story can seem, and how far you can string them along until it falls apart. Reading mail about a passenger complaint or other such violation can be a good release. The thing is, with Muni, the truth is actually far more interesting than anything anyone could ever make up! If you can't get 'em rolling in the receiver's area, then good luck in rolling down Mission for the next nine or ten hours! Don't worry, something worthy of next day's receiver's room banter will probably come up!

If on the extra board, runs are assigned daily, and can be checked after 2:30 p.m. in the room where the schedule detail is posted. Comparing cap number seniority to assigned runs can also add to drama. We then sign on our run on the operator's sign-in sheet, and look for the coach assigned to our run on the track assignment, and note the number down on our paddle. Sometimes, the words, *See the yard-starter* are on the sign-in sheet, and we have to go down to the tower to find out what coach number we are to be assigned. Rather than going out in the yard with the sinking feeling of re-enacting a scene from *Maze Runner*, getting a new coach is a piece of cake. All the older trolleys were finally removed from the yard in preparation for the New Flyer trolleys which are undergoing testing to be augmented on the 30 Stockton and 5 Fulton lines.

In the tower, we state our run and line and ask for a coach. Sometimes we get to go on a walk with the yard-starter and find a coach. This is often necessary at Potrero, as coaches are coming and going continuously. I have had the unique coming or going vibe as I would pull-in at 2:44 a.m. from the 14 Mission, and I see the yard-starter and receiver starting their day getting ready for the next shift of early day run operators. *Are you coming or going?* is perhaps the number one question I get asked.

I have not needed to purchase much in the way of civilian clothing, as I wear my uniform as a part of my body, up to 15 hours a day! Just like our trolleys, we are "in service" most of our waking life! Go up to any Muni operator and ask them the last time they bought any regular clothes. Or ask them the last time they wore something other than the uniform! You'll probably get a laugh. And if you don't, please *s-l-o-w-l-y* move away and carry on! Do not ask any more questions!

Such as in pulling-in from Daly City at 2:21 in the morning. If you see an operator engaged with another passenger, such as assisting a drunk sleeper on the back steps, wait to ask about where to stand to catch the next bus. Even if the owl coach has been parked in the terminal for several minutes, allow the operator of the next bus to clear the coach first.

Also important to remember is the rule that I must walk to the back of the coach to check all seats before I pull into see next morning's yard-starter. If a youth has fallen asleep in the seats near the back, or by the articulated joint in the double-long coach, I cannot see them from my interior rear view mirror.

I was blessed to have an inspector checking pull-ins from Bryant and 16th to call for assistance to have a youth removed who would not wake up or stir from his slumped over position. It can take up to an hour to have the police and then the fire department remove an intoxicated person on a stretcher in an ambulance off to San Francisco General Hospital. It is a no-no to pull-in and leave a surprise for the car cleaner!

So seeing a yard-starter when I pull-out, and then in the wee hours of the morning when I pull-in, makes this well rounded Muni operator a guidepost to the start of my day, and sometimes the last good-bye as I go home. When I see a yard-starter willing to drop and rack poles in the yard and help coaches pull out on time, I know I am in for a good sign-up!

Another tally for finding the Zen and keeping my job if I can see them in the yard and walk off without going upstairs to fill out an incident report!

First Stop

WHEN I PULL OUT IN the morning, I always smile and say hello to my first customer. I try to make this an important barometer for how the day will go. And it gives me an instant check-in to see where I am at in my head, and whether or not I am present to be of service. Yes, the job gives great paychecks, but I have always followed the precept that do what you like and the money will follow. Even though I believe most city employees think more about their paycheck than the service they provide to get it, I do know placing service first is actually my best action to create job security.

I am surprised to admit I may not be following this belief for more than half the time I spend behind the wheel. Or at least I am not aware that I am. Most of my actions become subconscious, which is great from a Zen point of view, but it takes considerable effort to get back to a service first mode when I am running late and heavy.

So the great thing about the first stop and the first passenger is that none of burdens of being late or overwhelmed, exist, usually. And I always try to find a start time that doesn't put me behind the eight ball from the get go.

There are certain quirks in the schedule that place cut-in coaches at a disadvantage at the first terminal. Usually it because the leader is late and ends up being behind the cut-in coach where the new coach begins service. And so at the first terminal, the pull-out 'leader' has to pull poles to let the follower regain leader headway.

Headway is the time between buses. A leader is the bus scheduled on the paddle (timetable) in front of me. With the cuts to recovery time

(time allowed at a terminal) the leader may not have any wiggle room to relax and recover before heading out from the terminal.

And so, I have learned to cut in at not necessarily the exact time, but to make sure my leader passes before I cut in. Sometimes it is easier to trail blaze ahead and keep the follower less busy so he can make better time to arrive at the next terminal with some recovery time. All these nuances do influence how I feel when I get to my first terminal, and hence, shorten or lengthen my temper when picking up those first few passengers at the first stop.

I found out I am not a rush hour downtown bus driver. I am a crosstown guy who avoids being on that inbound trip at 8:30 a.m. or that 5:15 p.m. trip outbound. Crosstown is where it's at for me. The Muni meaning behind "doing homework" means checking out the paddles to see where the run is in the morning and in the afternoon. Paddles are the individual timetable for each bus driver's run. You can usually see this on the visor above the operator. People always ask me what the bad line is. I say there are no bad lines. Only bad leaving times.

Not all Stops are Equal

WHEN BUSES ARE MISSING, THE time between buses doubles so waiting time increases. It can become very unclear to those standing at or near multiple line bus stops why the bus passes by. The bus is full because double headway means double passenger load.

One phrase used frequently by bus drivers are the phrases, "my time" and "your people." Such as, "He left on my time," or "I am picking up her people." The tone in which this is said is in proportion to the tension felt by those waiting. Use of a Jerry Springer Show dialect, with a sliding bobble head neck drives home the point of coming to work to do work, or to just stay home.

All the frantic yelling and screaming is moot if you are no longer in the scanning range of the operator or outside the zone. The scanning range of an operator is one to two blocks ahead of the direction of travel. Once the front door passes by where you stand, lucky is the day the bus stops. And I do appreciate your thanks when I do stop. But stopping is the exception to the rule when I am late and I am full.

If no one rings to get off, and the bus is full, the bus doesn't stop. It becomes important to see how full a bus is as it approaches. Looking away on a cell phone, or talking to someone else and facing away from the direction of travel, all compound the chance of a bus not stopping if no request to stop is made on board on a crowded bus. These are the unwritten rules of not wanting a bus: If you are not facing the operator as the bus is a half a block away, and you are alone, and you are on Van Ness or Mission, we usually will not stop. In San Francisco there are so many passing by, or standing, or sleeping (or

12

whatever) in the shelter, we have learned to look at your hands to see if you are holding the fare. This is called looking for those who are ready.

So baby stops, not at a light, or far side from the cross street, are not equal to major transfer points nearside at a stop light. Increasing your odds for pickup become relevant if no bus is seen coming, or you see the taillights of a bus just having gone by.

A red light can save you when headway is long, or a bus is full. A good question to ask yourself while waiting, is, what are the chances of someone wanting to get off at this stop where I am waiting? It also pays to be aware of when the next bus is due. Do you have a clock in the shelter where you are waiting? If not, is there another bus stop a block or two away that does have next bus? If you are waiting at a minor stop with no clock, and no way to see a bus coming, should you move to a better line-of-sight stop by a stop light or transfer point, so as to increase the chances of a stop? The answer is Yes!

Odd numbered street stops have been removed in the Inner Mission to reduce dwell time and running time for the 14 line and this makes it important to know where to stand and have your pass ready to tag-in with your phone or card. As soon as you leave the store with your wallet out, get ready to have your phone or fare ready to go. This compliments our 'red carpet' treatment on the pavement: transit gets priority over car traffic. The newly painted red lane reduces congestion from the influx of the 5,000 ride share cars coming into the city from the East Bay.

If, however, that other stop has a large number of people waiting, sometimes it pays to backtrack to a stop with less people waiting so you can get a better spot inside the bus before it gets too full. Giving up a major stop is good if you can tell on your smartphone or the shelter next bus time clock, that another bus is only one or two minutes behind the first coach. Usually this first bus is packed, and the next one is okay. So sometimes getting on the first bus is bad.

The chances of a fight breaking out, "Quit Pushing!" "Get off my Leg!" and such always occurs on the first, more crowded bus. The chances of this bus going out of service are also greater.

Think about it. When you see a mob of people getting off of a bus that stops working, it is a mob of people. Very rarely is it an un-crowded bus. This crowded bus is usually late and arrives after a long wait for buses. Try to avoid getting caught by noticing how many people are waiting when you first arrive on foot to the bus stop. Sometimes if you get on a local neighborhood bus or another line with less people, you can transfer later down the line and be on time.

So what am I saying? I am saying if you are smoking a cigarette, talking on your cell phone, looking away from the street, all alone or sitting down, and look like you haven't seen the inside of a gym in years, forget about it! All the shouting and cursing in the world isn't going to make the bus stop, unless you can beat it to the next red light and get the cap number of the bus driver! Good Luck, and see you next time!

The Fare Box

SURVEYS OF TIME USE SHOW much time is spent in the bus zone loading passengers. Although this would seem to be a revenue loser as those who board in the rear would be evading the fare, my experience has been most riders are honest and pay their fare share by coming to the front door to get a receipt or transfer. Those who enter in the back because of wheelchair boarding or kneeler requests, do come to the front from the aisle to get a transfer, and pay their fare. By believing most people are honest and abide by the unofficial honor system of paying for their ride, I have reduced almost all problems and delays at the front door and fare box.

This surrender on my part has made my job a lot easier, and I always try to be of service if someone is a little short, but needs a ride. This took me several years of discovery, as I am somewhat of a perfectionist. My Mars in Aries has reared its ugly head with some fare disputes that got me into trouble. And the idea the riders also can train operators by their feedback, even if it is unpleasant. Being rude or appearing nasty is a fast behavior modify if ever there was one. How riders react to my statement of what the fare is, over time, gives me an idea of how I am to handle myself, or set the tone of requesting the fare, without getting into an argument.

The obvious dilemma one first realizes as a transit operator, is how oblivious passengers are in expecting us to see their fare in the first place. If I had one wish to click my heels to make come true, it would be for boarders to see how impossible it is for us to check their fare. If it were a problem with less than 10 percent of people riding, then it would seem like I am being picky or controlling, but over half of the people boarding do not show their fare in what I would call a thoughtful or honest way. Granted, as two columns of people board at major transfer points, they pass by quickly if I am lucky, but the way in which I am to look at their fast pass or transfer is ridiculous by any standard. By injecting humor into the situation by stating there are two lines, fast track and exact change, and motioning to imaginary two lines at the front door helps interrupt the pattern of blocking that occurs from tagging in on the one side, and the fare box on the other.

So there should be no surprise why the majority of operators appear to not be looking at the fare when it is presented. Almost no one appears to be concerned we have a chance to actually look at their hand. I'd say less than one in ten boarders actually shows me the fare in a reasonable way. I've learned if I turn in my seat to face the door, and appear genuinely interested in looking at what's in your hand, then odds do increase for proper fare presentation.

What the majority don't seem to understand is that front door boarding is no reason for a reduction in fare evasion. People showing fare properly at the front door are such a small fraction of the total, that to us as operators, it makes no difference what door people enter. Hopefully with the newer cameras, if anyone is actually viewing images, they would see it virtually impossible to see most fares, even at the front door.

This brings us to the various styles of impossibility of "fare evasion" by those coming to the front door. Once again, what I have just said is contrary to the start of this Chapter when I said most people are honest, and abide by the unofficial honor system. There seems to be a paradox. And indeed there is. While I said most people are honest in paying the fare, I also said they are clueless about how useless their presentation is, for us to see. And bereft of knowing what they are showing, after countless times being berated by them for questioning their fare, taking my request personally such as an attack on their character, I have learned how to ask for the fare without too much backwash. So here are some of the major "food groups" of fare evasion. Remember, I am not saying these passengers don't actually have a valid fare. What I am saying, is for the purpose of checking the fare, these maneuvers constitute fare evasion because we cannot determine if the fare has been paid.

The Wand

Like Merlin the magician, or something out of a Harry Potter movie, these people move their arm in such a wide swath it is a miracle anyone can see what the hell it is they are holding. We have many types of pass ID acceptable for fare, but it doesn't matter, because we can't see what the hell it is people are showing us anyway. This does not mean we should not make an effort to look at people's hands when they board, and it definitely does not mean we should just rationalize into not checking at all.

A hard working driver was asked by a man why he wasn't asking for the fare for those who boarded in the rear, and he replied that they do it all the time. He got written up for a passenger service request (PSR) because this is against the rule that we ask for the fare by stating what the adult fare is. He could have asked to see the fare of those boarding in the rear or by making the announcement to please come to the front if you need to pay your fare, but he didn't.

These small nuances can come at any time at any place, and we have to be ready to do the right thing. If we get distracted by another question, or are in our mind about something else, these small rituals throw us off and we get mail. We get a letter for a review about our behavior when we can't see why this is so.

If we talk to other drivers about this at the relief point or in the receivers office, we usually get the right answer. I would rarely ask for help or feedback when I was new, and this added years of distress that did not really need to be there. So when the wand goes by, we need to always be ready to do the correct action. Ask for the fare,

17

even if the person whipping by us never stops. Most times, the wrong person usually stops to question us. "No, I wasn't asking you. The fare is two dollars twenty five cents." And that's usually the end of it. Just as in calling out transfers and destinations, it matters not the right person hears us. Just that we were following the rule.

Our most honorable Mayor, Mr. Gavin Newsom, when riding on a cable car, made the observation that the conductor was not checking fares. What he may not have known, is we become accustomed to our regulars. We know who has their fast pass, and after the fourth of the month, it is not necessary to see the fast pass every day. Just because it is not apparent that we are checking every fare, does not mean we do or do not know who is paying.

The Jack-knife

In all fairness, there are those seniors, and those with mobility problems that may make coming up the stairs a balancing act. I have to be mindful of being of service, especially towards those with mobility problems that may not be visible, however, can we at least make an attempt, once in a blue moon, to at least show the operator that we have a current valid monthly pass? If the month is new, and we are a regular, isn't it reasonable to show the operator at the beginning of the month that we have our new pass?

The jack-knife is accomplished like the wand except for an excessive up and down motion with the arm holding the pass. Made to look like the arm is a counterweight to the balancing act of climbing, there is no chance in hell our eyes can focus on a pass that is moving up and down at or near the speed of light. Just because you are holding the pass does not mean we have the ability to see it.

When I explain that this is the fourth of the month, and many old passes have expired, this usually helps. If a regular rider becomes offended that I am asking to see their fare, I respond by saying, "Yes, I know you are a regular pass holder, but I haven't seen you with the new pass yet." If the fourth day of the new month is after a holiday, I give grace for this. "Are you going to get your new one today?" Then things get better. "You need this transfer until you purchase your new pass, I don't want you to get in trouble." This heals all wounds, and prevents me from being perceived as a heal. The great reward at first impressions was when days turned into weeks turned into months, without anyone taking my fare checking personally. This took me over five years to be able to say this truthfully.

Toll Booth

Having been a Jersey boy, I pride myself on being quick to pay toll. If you have ever been headed to points south from NYC on the Garden State Parkway on a summer weekend, and you have successfully crossed the Raritan River Bridge crossing and toll booth, you know how paying the toll in the bucket in a timely fashion can contribute to delays of those behind you. Before the days of automatic billing, knowing how to do the toll booth was an art.

The one thing about Californian's laid backness which some times drives my east coast roots up the wall, is the sense of cluelessness about how action or in this case inaction has a cannonball affect on others. I have never met a native New Yorker who was completely clueless at the fare box.

Granted, I may be able to teach them about the waterfall method as an enhancement of toll booth, but some Californians who have grown complacent and accustomed to not showing their fare, are the biggest offenders with the toll booth method of fare payment. Should they be asked to show their fare by the fare inspector, they become grudging payers. They may be seasoned riders, but it fast becomes obvious at the box they are unfamiliar with actually paying a cash fare.

This is where I have to get over myself. I need to remember everyone is doing the best they can, given what they know and what they have.

And my judgment of others as a silent arrogance remains with me today. Try as I might to maintain humility, I quickly fall back into self-centered superiority, thinking that I am the boss, and that I am in charge. And I find I lose my balance, and fall back into a familiar pattern of not liking you if you don't behave like I think you should.

The toll booth method involves dropping the coins over the slot in a dropping fashion, using the thumb or pointer finger as the feeder for the coin drop. Most people take the slow drip method instead of the fast pour because they are counting out their fare as they pay. This method is a bummer on morning peak inbounds if people haven't counted out their change in advance. This really slows us down and is the best reason to eliminate the fare altogether.

Dump Truck

These folks have learned a single coin drop by drop is too slow, so they count their change ahead of time. This is a great first step to making the step-up flow. But dropping the whole wad at once plugs up the coin slot. And those who have perfected this style usually also know how to fish with their fingers to stir the pile and let the coins trickle past the slot. But I need to be willing to show them how to clear the slot. And if they aren't willing to wait to see this, I need to surrender and clear the pile anyway.

What I resist, persists. And so I need the humility to wait another day to find the right time to see if they will learn. After all, their rush to move back is my desire. I have to see my part in creating the dump truck. This patience to resist change upon them is something I have to constantly guard against in picking up folks who are slow to the door placement. And if I don't allow them the grace to do their thing, trouble soon follows.

So I review my day and make sure I don't resist what I fear is to be a constant unchanging dilemma upon my daily trips. And with tourists or first timers. If I am short and without patience, the sooner I can catch myself the better. And God, or the transit gods, do give me grace in making a mistake once or twice. But if I go unchecked, and don't do a daily review, an incident will invariably occur whereby my being wrong comes back to bite. So, I need to be clear when a coin dropper has counted their fare, this as a first step in the right direction on my part.

And I do get rewarded when I see the dump truck method working. Especially with dimes. Dimes are the worst for jamming. If I create a patient and loving attitude when a jam occurs, the situation rarely repeats itself. The more I resist, the more frequent the jam. And the problem won't go away until I surrender.

Tissue Deluxe

I was always seeing granny holding her fare in a wrap of tissue. And the tissue would breakup and fall into the coin slot and lead to a coin bypass. Or there was some hair that fell into the coin slot along with the coins. Hopefully, I could dump the whole lot with my dump button and make the problem go away. But over time, if not caught right away, the fare box would stop counting coins, and the coins would build in the neck and cause a constant distraction.

It wasn't until I asked why seniors would wrap their coins that I got the answer. Their hands were dry with age, and the coins would stick to their palm and not go in. They had learned to put the coins in a wrap so that they would not stick to their skin, and go in. They were only trying to be ready and be fast, but I didn't see it this way. So whenever I see something happening over and over which is not to my liking, if I stop to ask, I get my answer and the distraction goes away. Finding the right time and place to get the answer doesn't occur when I think it should. Only after I take a prayerful pause to be ready to accept I may not have the answer, does the answer soon come. And the sooner the answer comes, the closer to being mentally fit am I.

This gets me excited about my job again. If I take the role of a detective, and try to unravel a mystery, I am back in the right mind set to discover the answer. And the answer is not one of arrogance or hostility to make my life as a driver miserable, but because they are only trying to do the right thing after having problems paying the fare the regular way with their palm and fingers. Most operators are not so controlling as I am, so they haven't had to worry about how someone pays the fare. But for me it was a big deal. I am not a good person if I ignore what I thought to be the most important deal for keeping my employer in the black by collecting as much fare as possible.

In reality, this tightrope actually was reducing my job security and my paycheck as I was being perceived as a dick, or a mean driver. So the comment, all conflict arises from misplaced desire, really hit home here. I am not the gestapo or the police. I am not an inspector. I am simply required to state what the fare is and let it go. Passengers actions or reactions are not my responsibility. And once I got over this, my job at the fare box got easier.

Dollar Curl

I have always had a recurrent idea in a dream state regarding a life purpose here. And it revolves around a seemingly impossible task such as in *Horton Hears a Who*, whereby the elephant has to go through a field of flowers to find the one flower with the one speck containing Who-ville. The enemy drops the one single flower into a huge field of flowers off of a cliff. Amazingly, our hero begins the daunting task without a single hesitation.

In my design, it is like cleaning up a huge trashed-out area like a stadium after a game, or trying to change a mass behavior, engrained on such a large scale, so no one person would ever agree to start picking the first flower, the first piece of trash, the one request from another person because the immensity of the task at hand is huge. But that my goal or purpose in life, is to begin the impossible task, and to be successful in the task with someone coming by later to remark, "You're done already? I can't believe it!"

I have had some success in this area. Except for the dollar curl, Transit operation does seem to offer the ultimate challenge. To change a behavior that is creating some delay or headache, and to make it largely disappear. I would hope to borrow Dante's wisdom: from the little spark may burst a mighty flame. Not the spark of a fare dispute creating a brush fire of anger, but like that of a candle in a cathedral, spreading light to an entire congregation. Such that the problem is basically removed forever. Everyone understands how to put a worn bill in the meter. And having the knowledge I was there at the beginning. That one person can actually make a difference. That it isn't about the impossibility of ever finishing, but about be willing to try. And see what happens. And so I trudge with the dollar curl.

Not all fare boxes are created equal. I found out from a co-worker in the revenue department that the slots on some of the bill meters are narrower. I would always take the effort to make a revenue appointment for my coach and see what I could learn. It seems few operators would ever consider calling Central Control to get a fare box fixed while in revenue service, but I did so anyway.

I learned something about what causes the fare box to fail: hair in the coin slot, tobacco and cotton and cotton from pockets that were mixed with the coins; and just the regular dust on dollars. But I also learned about what to look for that would set the ball in motion to begin to clog the fare box. And my problems of fare box failure went down.

I would get owl coaches assigned to me in the morning from another run, I would go through a period of days where I would get several coaches in a row that had bad fare boxes. But if I kept calling to get revenue to meet me at Ferry Plaza, or Cal train, or Howard and New Montgomery, I learned where the good times and places were to ask to meet. I never would have figured this out if I never called. And around 9 a.m. in an off peak direction, by the inbound terminal, where other coaches collected, was a good time and place.

So my journey about cause began. Then on to offer help when and where the problem started. When someone put a dollar or coin into the box. If a dollar has a bent up corner, or if the edge is creased, the dollar will not go in on fare boxes with a narrow slot. So if I had a box like this, I knew it would be a problem. This would be a problem on about one in three coaches. And it became easier to look at their bill before they put it in the slot, rather than to watch them struggle and hold up the boarding cue. Saying to them to flip it over didn't work because they would try the other side of the bill rather than a simple flip, and the other side had a crease up in the same direction. Using my hand as an example doesn't work because they are focusing not on my hand but on the slot. Telling them to crease the bill in the middle lengthwise results in them folding it in half which acts as a dam in the machine, and increases chances for a jam. Stating that a bent up crease doesn't work because they are in a hurry to get by as we have trained them to do, so showing them how to put it in is the fastest and best. Most don't care, or seem interested in knowing this, but over time, I noticed fewer and fewer people having problems.

I started seeing more people with worn bills having them pre-folded to put into the machine. I also learned from them that two bills together work, and that other operators had told them about how to crease the bill before putting it in the slot. So by using my hand in a curl, pointing my fingers down, stating that the dollar moves into the machine going down through the roller, I saw the light go off in their head, and declared it another victory of the day. Because even though I may never see that person again, I could take comfort knowing that on some other bus somewhere else, a driver was able to make the light, or close the door just a little sooner, because that one extra person was ready at the fare box.

The Question

These are the pros. They don't have the fare, and usually don't intend to pay, but by framing the greet by asking a question about where I go, they get me to tell them the correct answer, and they thank me passing without showing a fare. They have made me look good. Doing service. They get to pass by without a delay. And there isn't any humiliating or hostile story about asking or needing a ride. And I have since gotten less offended at the those who do the drive by. That is, those who don't look, talk, or indicate that they have a fare, but use the others paying their fare as a smoke screen to passing by without fare. But after realizing I am here to be of service in providing a ride, I became less angry at the drive by folks, because, in the end, they were saving me time in the zone. Do you need a transfer? is the best one liner to get their attention and see if they have some money to put in the box. Some times they only have a penny to put in. I'll take it. Hey, it's one penny more than Muni would have got. And the sense of self esteem that seems to manifest from this does seem to make for a friendlier coach and a friendlier ride. Better than those who ask the question are those who say. . .

"I Have It."

Free Ride

FOR THOSE RIDERS WHO ARE ready, a free ride is an opportunity to imagine what Muni would be like with no fare box at all. A smile and thank you is all it takes as a regular breezes by the yellow line to find a seat. The Zen zone is strong and the crunch zone seems *A long time ago in a galaxy far, far away.* Now is the time it becomes easy to spot those who have not mastered how to ride the bus in San Francisco.

I can put the defect card over the bill meter or clipper tag-in device with the words, *Free Ride, Clipper not working.* But this is not enough for those intent on paying a fare without the casual greater awareness of what is going on around them. Their tunnel vision is restricting their ability to learn and adapt to changing conditions around them. This can be fear based, or newcomer based. Either way, the free ride benefit of saving dwell time in the zone is completely lost upon these folks. I must find my Zen to minimize this loss of time and distraction. Usually hand signals work best. Waving my hand over the fare box and motioning to step past works best. I was able to get my Muni Diaries audience to practice this at my performance as Driver Doug!

They all started to make the waterfall motion as I kept repeating the motion over and over on stage. Ninety nine percent of intending cash fare boarders get it, even though they may pause to create brief bumper cars with the person behind them attempting to stick the dollar under the defect card. Or they attempt to tag over and over and over and over again. Chinese seniors are the number one record holder of consecutive tags on clipper when the system is not working.

When clipper is off, and no sound emits from speaker, I can praise Tibetan Monks, Allah, or Prime Creator!

Being spiritual helps when a wardrobe malfunction occurs in lifting up a shirt or jacket with the pass on a lanyard around the neck. Or with a hip check running into the person 'next door' also trying to pay the fare. Creating a fast track lane and an exact change lane by motioning with hand signals from my seat at a big stop brings smiles of relief from the crowd. *Step Up Please! Exact change on the right, Clipper on the left!* And the Zen of knowing *when* to use the two lane step up!

Those in the shop at the tower or on air at central control very rarely contain the empathy of what life is like for hours on end in the cockpit when something not safety significant is not working properly, or intermittent. At the end of the day, it's not whether our request is heeded on the defect card, but rather how we let such a distraction become an entertainment. The *musts* of demonstrating the patience of a Muni bus driver can come into play even in a free ride situation as their are those determined to pay a fare no matter what. Perhaps they just got dinged by a fare inspector. Maybe they have a strong resentment against those that do not show their fare and cheat the system, and they be damned if they board without a beep. Interestingly, this group is just as confounding as those that fumble without fare at the front door blocking the steps. *If you don't have your card out and need to ask a question, let others at the stop, who are ready, go first.*

If you are a coach pulling-in, it never hurts to ask for a transfer when you get off. Back door boarders have this one down. Because the coach is a short line coach, a new transfer with more time is usually given. We cannot waste transfers and may have longer ones already cut. Whether you got on for free or not is not the pressing matter. What is on our mind as an operator is to go home! *I forgot to get a transfer when I got on.* This works great instead of the hostile name calling, going out the back door empty-handed. The next regular coach is usually right behind the short line pull-in coach, and if you are fast at exiting the front door, you can get a new transfer. Being polite and respectful to the operator pays dividends for a free ride, especially if my momma is not involved in your request.

So the free ride should become fun and easy. A smile and a nod is all it takes. If someone continues to dump coins or wedge a faded dollar in the slot, I can become Austin Powers, Church Lady, or O'be Wan Kanobi. *Oh behave. Could it be Satan? May the Force Be With You.* Or the English Church version: *Peace Be With You.*

Tag-in Please

SAN FRANCISCO TROLLEYS NOW HAVE a tag-in device located to the left of all doors as you enter. Now in credit card form, as a plastic Clipper card, monthly fast passes, cash, and other forms of fare can be discarded with a quick swipe or tag in at the door. Right. Sure. And now all forms of fare evasion are healed. Not quite. But I could see early on that this technology, once it caught on and became familiar with the masses, boarding would be made much easier. Only problem, was in the learning curve of the first phase of passengers and operators to become aware of the nuances of using this clipper card so as to keep the flow when boarding.

I knew there would be problems, and so when some problem kept coming up frequently, I would choose those moments when Zen pervaded the coach and my attention, to ask the passenger what was going on with their card when an unsuccessful tag was being shown on my dashboard screen. I found out that there were delays in crediting payment. Those with multiple agency payments, such as BART and Muni, had to tag in more than once to verify ID. If a person was pay as you go on BART, and had the Non BART Fast Pass monthly pass on Muni, their card would read as blocked or low funds unless they tagged in again. And being quick to judge someone was evading fare has never worked for me at the fare box, so I was sure I would take this tag-in message as not necessarily correct with regards to correct payment. Being wrong at first blush creates an added emotional hassle with passenger relations that need not be.

If I took the position in my mind that all passengers were trying to get one over on the new system, and that they intentionally knew that they were trying to get on free, things would not go well, and I would learn nothing. In those rare cases when a boarder tried to explain something, or ask a question about the clipper card, I stayed open to find out what the history was behind their getting the card, and why their card was not beeping normally. Sure enough, when a card had two different payment forms from two different agencies, a second tag was needed. The card reader could only read one payment form at a time, and the default read may not be correct. Also there were delays in payment credit with the cards. Just because someone went to pay their bill online or at a convenience store, did not mean it would read correctly at the gate instantly.

Aside from the low funds messages, there were other non-payment warnings. "Blocked" and "not-permitted" were two other messages that were warning of non-payment. When in Zen, I waited to choose my battles wisely. I found out what was really going on. "Not Permitted" was from a passenger who purchased a paper card reader from the underground metro system and had already tagged a second time on a surface coach. The paper card issued from the underground system would not allow a pass back message after one transfer had been used. This jibed with what I knew about the older turn style receipts issued before the new gate system was installed. "Blocked" came up when a card was reported lost or stolen, or a newer card by the holder was issued. And then I found out why people had more than one card in their wallet. The problem was when they had more than one card in their wallet, and they tagged–in without taking a single card out of their billfold, the system went down or sounded a loud alarm. Then, they tagged in again and everything was okay. I couldn't figure out why this happened.

I found out the second tag was from another card. I started looking at what they were doing when the second tag was okay. Getting the mirrors just right took some doing because most folks would block a direct view of seeing where their hands and card was by standing between me and the reader. New people were the best at showing me what they were doing. Blocking my view is a characteristic of fare evaders, so it took some doing to find out if blocking my view was intentional or not. So by asking those who were open and friendly, I found out they carried two cards because they were having problems with low funds warnings on the first tag-in. They also realized having more than one payment option from two separate agencies like BART or Cal Train, or the Ferry systems, created problems with the tag-in.

So now I had most of the reasons why a bad tag-in was occurring, and why there were plausible reasons why the passenger did not know why an error was occurring, I could move on to the problem of people bumping into one another when they paid the fare and moved back down the aisle.

"Fast track on the right, please. Clipper on the left. Please form two lines." This is a good announcement to make at big stops and transfer points to get the flow going and reduce boarding times. Exact change folks at the fare box to the right of the steps, and Clipper card taggers to the left of the steps gets two lines going and cuts down zone delays in half. Anytime I can reduce dwell time in the zone, my Zen zone increases, and my day is a good one.

Where to Stand

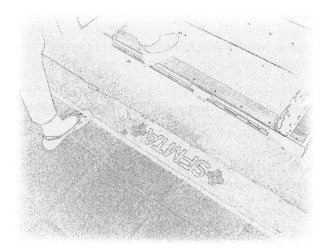

MOST OF THE TIME INTENDING passengers are not standing where I want to place the front doors. Folks don't seem to understand what it takes for a forty foot or sixty foot vehicle to come to the curb, and then have enough room to pull away leaving a four foot clearance from any object or vehicle parked nearby at the head of the zone. If pressed for time, I can always do a flag stop. A flag stop is when I keep the bus parallel in the traffic lane and drop the kneeler to have folks step off of the curb and come to the door. Only problem is, if there are those waiting who have mobility problems, not coming to the curb is also a problem. Using the "body english" of the coach, I can control how long I spend in the zone, and where folks must migrate to get to the door.

If I am early, I can make people walk a distance on the sidewalk to come to my door, which may not be where the majority are standing.

If I am late, I can flag the stop, and pull away faster because I have clear visibility to the rear in my mirrors because my bus is straight, and I can see far back to see approaching cars. Problem is, when I am late, I am usually heavy, and have standing room only. This is when flagging a stop and not coming to the curb may be a problem because usually seniors are present, and the kneeler may groan in trying to rise after I pick up because the aisle is full, and the bus is heavy. Use of the kneeler can damage the suspension and cause a fall on board.

So a rule of thumb that some operators may not have experience to pick up on, and what most passengers seem to be amiss about, is the painted stencil on the red curb, usually between the two MTA stars, that says "bus stop."

These stencils I have found, are accurately placed as the best place to put the front door. The stencils are roughly the distance between the two sets of doors. I don't understand the coincidence of this, and why it works so well, but this is generally the case. I have had issues with where the various stencils are placed to mark our breakers and switches on the street, but the bus stop markers are highly accurate. So if you want to "be the man," or the "woman" who gets to be the first on the bus, here is what you can do to increase the odds that the bus stops where you are.

When the bus is one block away, and say, gets a green light at the corner before the stop, slowly wave your arm from beside your leg to a point halfway up or perpendicular to your stance, back and forth, when the bus starts to move a block away. If you are standing mid way from the top of the zone to the first stencil on the red curb, and there are no double parked cars at the head of the zone, or encroached upon the zone rectangle in the street, you are a "winner." The bus will stop right where you are standing and you can be the first to board, especially if you have your pass or card visible in your hand when the bus approaches. Kudos and good karma, you've got the Zen in San Francisco transit!

Morning Rush

WE ALL KNOW WE TRY to cut it as close as we can and get away without wasting any time. This image of efficiency is to take the bus without any waiting time. But just like a *Mad* magazine comic strip, if we are all making the same determinations at the same time, we invariably create our own hell.

What I came to believe from the run from hell, was to note at what time was the point of no return for folks not able to make it the elevator to work before the clock strikes nine. And I found, down to the minute, that someone walking out their door at 8:22 a.m. in the avenues of 22 and 23, could not make it to work in time downtown. The last express just passed by at 8:21 a.m., and my coach would fill to the brim before I even got to Park Presidio, which is around 14th Avenue. If someone walked out their door by 8:15 a.m. they stood a chance to make it to work on time, but they were still risking it.

Indeed, the window of vulnerable time was actually about six minutes, which coincidentally was the headway between coaches, and that this time window seemed, at first, to be a plausible time to allow for getting downtown. It seems reasonable to make it downtown in 42 minutes from 22nd Avenue.

But not when the Muni system is challenged to peak capacity, when many are traveling in the same direction at the same time, to get to a destination within a few blocks of each other. The many new tall buildings downtown have made a mess of trying to catch a bus after 8:20 a.m. from the Avenues or from beyond Masonic Avenue. Pass-ups become frequent during this time frame as there is simply just not enough capacity to bring that large of a swarm of people at once to work by 9 a.m. on the dot.

And so I started looking at the passenger loads of buses that were to arrive downtown by 9 a.m. And sure enough, the passenger load was very telling. A bus arriving downtown at 9:15 a.m. or 9:22 a.m. was much emptier than one scheduled to arrive on or before 9 a.m.

But crosstown routes were another matter. Crosstown coaches were less influenced by the peak period flux, but their drop offs at transfer points were critical for inbound downtown coaches.

My leader, god bless him, was able to "escape" past the transfer points before those coaches dropped off their passengers trying to transfer to get downtown. And this "transfer cost" had a lot to do whether people could make it to work on time, or whether they stood waiting for a downtown bound coach already too crowded to take on any new transfer passengers. But I also came to believe it might be impossible for scheduling to try to take all this in account and place extra buses during this witching hour.

The bottom line I came to realize is if individuals found they could not make the trip in a timely fashion, they would have to move-up at least ten or twenty minutes to avoid the bind. The supposed injustice of this model is that at some point after 8 a.m., the time it would take to get where you needed to go, was much longer than someone leaving the house at, say, 7:30 a.m. And so, if there was some magic wand I could wave to business leaders to make the perception of transit doing its job and running on time, it would be to stagger work start times in 15 minute increments, so that no one large group of people would be required to clock in at one specific time.

The patterns of going home do seem to support this idea. I noticed although the start time for people going to work was relatively cut and dried, the time people leave work is spread out over a longer time frame, as people may do other tasks before they get on the bus, such as staying at work a little bit longer. Also, because there was no deadline to get home in the afternoon as there was to get to work in the morning, this more relaxed attitude helped make a better environment for the bus driver in the p.m. rush. Usually.

And my tip to those up and comers working downtown, or to those looking to ask for a raise: show up early and get more work done when the office is quiet. Relax towards the afternoon when everyone is just playing card games or surfing the web at their desks. You may find your ride on the bus is much more pleasant when not on the ball and chain schedule of those arriving downtown by nine a.m. I'll bet your productivity would skyrocket if you came in two hours early to get stuff done without constant distraction. Not every day, mind you, but you might be surprised at how much faster you go to sleep and how much easier your commute in the morning and afternoon might be if you stagger your self earlier.

In San Francisco we do have sort of a split workforce. Many traders in the market, or manning the screens for trades are set on East Coast time and so they arrive early to work, and get off around 3 p.m. These guys do seem a lot happier than the ball and chain nine to fivers. And when they get on the bus in the morning, sometimes with tie in hand, you can't always tell if they have had their coffee. But for those after 8 a.m., I would suggest that you get your coffee near your office if your breakfast routine is dragging you down before you go out the door. In any event, if your morning commute is not working, try something different. I have seen the creatures of habit who are just miserable. Those who are more adaptable seem to have a better go of it. And taking a Zen approach brings dividends.

Five Greens of Happiness

O GRASSHOPPER, THE FIVE GREENS of happiness are a wonder to behold when leaving Embarcadero Building Three at Davis and Sacramento on the 1 California! I was blessed with a leaving time of 4:58 p.m. and I could make it to Kearny at the foot of Chinatown before the masses descended from the downtown towers at 5 p.m. Begin my turn at 4:57 p.m., and I am gaining extra green lights, and five more blocks!

My follower turned into a major crybaby about leaving time, believing I was intentionally making his life hell by leaving early. My *escape velocity* with a leaving time only four minutes ahead of his 5:02 p.m., made a huge difference in passenger load. If I left one minute early, as I can do without getting in trouble, this made the difference in whether or not I could make the five greens of happiness: green lights at Davis, Front, Battery, Sansome, and Montgomery. If I had less than six people at Montgomery, I could make Kearny just as this light too, would turn green. Because I reached Montgomery at 5:04 p.m. or as late as 5:06 p.m., the number of intenders would change, and thus reduce predictability of a green at Kearny. *Hallelujah, Mother of Pearl*, this difference was not too fretful because I had passed the area of tall buildings on the flats.

The downtown area is built on the carcasses of old wooden vessels of all types. Boats were sunk and the bay was filled-in to create downtown as it now stands. Montgomery Street was on the old shoreline and you can detect this subtle difference as the land begins to rise from this point outbound. Chinatown's Portsmouth Square is on the old shoreline. This is where the shot heard round the world was made my US Army General Sheridan, *There's Gold in them hills!* This gold rush has been replaced by the daily outbound transit peak period rush away from work downtown!

All the small, old, brick turn of century buildings above Montgomery, are of a different era than the skyscrapers that shoot skyward from Montgomery all the way down to the Ferry Plaza. Commercial Alley is the last reminder of where the dock extended all the way out to where Ferry Plaza now stands. If you stand on Kearny at Commercial, and look to the new shoreline, you will see the first steel reinforced building of our city; and the clock tower atop the Ferry Building. Saving this view was intentional when designing the Embarcadero office complex.

The five Embarcadero buildings architects' genius included an open walkway between the towers, from Chinatown to Justin Herman Plaza, so the historic walkway remains. Designed in the mid-to-late 1960's, these five buildings proudly display their outlines with white Christmas lights during the holidays. They appear fresh and modern as any other newer building in town. The plaza tile is kept immaculate and looks like it was laid last year, even though this complex is now over forty years old.

Imitating computer chips or boards stacked vertically together in parallel staggered fashion, they presaged San Francisco's tech importance with a style and design that fits in perfectly today. You can look down Commercial from Chinatown and see the Ferry Building just as you can see it when you look down Market Street from the Union Square area. Indeed, one of the joys of being a transit operator is the breathtaking beauty that appears in many places on many lines.

On the 1 California, seeing sunrise at Jones and Clay on Nob Hill as the street plunges to the old shoreline, energizes a gratitude of living in one of the most beautiful cities in the world. My other favorite vistas on Muni are seeing Alcatraz at Leavenworth on the 45 Union. Alignment of the penitentiary view with Leavenworth Street may be a coincidence hard to ignore from an inmate's view! Cresting Lone Mountain inbound on the 5 Fulton at the University of San Francisco at sunrise is also breathtaking. Saint Ignatius' twin towers stand majestic to be seen for miles around. The crosstown routes such as the 24 Divisadero have many such vistas: between Waller and Duboce as Castro Street becomes Divisadero, at Duncan and Noe, and at Jackson and Pierce. Atop Liberty Hill, the Castro can be seen inbound after crossing 22nd Street. The 22 Fillmore has a great panorama of the downtown skyline crossing 280 Freeway at Pennsylvania and 18th entering Dogpatch from Potrero Hill outbound. The alignment of the Sacred Heart tower on Fell is first glimpsed when passing Jackson and Fillmore after passing Mrs. Doubtfire's house on Steiner at Broadway. There are stunning views everywhere! With 43 hills over 49 square miles, a vista is never too far away.

Choosing a run on the 1 California in the afternoon with the Five Greens of Happiness is a blessing to behold and cemented my mastery of the Presidio Barn runs. For me, choosing the 30 Stockton in the morning and the 1 California in the afternoon was the smart choice. Doing the 1 in the morning and the 30 in the afternoon was not my cup of tea. Pass ups on the 1 and traffic on Third Street along with the trash trucks blocking a lane in Chinatown after 6 p.m. made for a long day.

All the produce refuse is collected on the last day shift trip on the 30 Stockton, and this can be a drag after a long 12 hour range. I timed this down to the minute when leaving Cal Train on Townsend. I had to leave on time not later than 41 minutes after the hour if I was to make Sacramento outbound before the first trash truck turned on to Stockton from Grant Street at 6:10 p.m. I am writing this chapter ten years after I did this run, and I still recall the time down to the minute! Chinatown is reduced to one lane if two opposing trash trucks are nearby and this can be intense. I quickly learned to put any stress I may encounter at the beginning of the shift such that as time wore on in the shift, things would get easier. Finding the Five Greens of Happiness was the final confirmation I had found Zen while driving a trolley!

Stopping and Starting

ONE OF THE MOST CHALLENGING aspects which takes its toll on the body is trying to maintain a smooth start and stop, particularly on a hill. All coaches are not equal. In order to maintain an even stop on a hill, some coaches require 40 to 60 percent more force on the pedal, and then, at 3 m.p.h., where the dynamic brake kicks-in, an abrupt off pedal feather to prevent a lurch.

Slack brakes are what cause the abrupt lurch after the air brake disengages right before the full stop. On a heavy day, with many hills, this can cause the calf or hamstring muscles to "complain." In order to keep hearing "thank you" when passengers alight, much torque force and muscle tension must be applied on a regular, staccato, repetitive manner. Sometimes we use the hill holder toggle to hold the bus instead of the service brake. This is a no-no.

As a passenger, especially if reading or texting, be mindful not to use the canvas hand-holds. This places you in an unstable mode. These loops are for sitting down or getting up only. If we start on a hill without first letting off of the service brake, you can feel the jerk. It is easy typing this information on a black and white manuscript to state that using the hill holder is not advised to release the brakes on a hill, but after hours and hours of double headway, fatigue sets-in. Our jerk is not necessarily from laziness, but of preservation of our quads and hamstrings.

If the time behind the seat is for more than four hours without a break, and you are missing a leader, this makes it difficult to walk up the stairs after work! Keeping my body from falling apart as I add on the mileage over the years of driving a bus is definitely a challenge to be able to stay at work and be in the Zen zone!

The Noodle

ONE OF THE NICEST TRICKS to leaving the zone safely at a nearside bus stop is what my line trainer called the noodle. If done correctly, it reduces squeeze play merging, and the set up for this maneuver helps prevent sideswipes caused by lack of visibility from the rear as a car approaches, particularly if a car is turning right to pass the coach.

I had trouble in spelling maneuver, so I looked it up in my dictionary. My Webster's Ninth New Collegiate Dictionary has several definitions (below) that fit this move. I have found it nice to have a dictionary handy when I write, because it clarifies what meaning I am trying to convey, and I take interest in all the other words I come across in trying to search for the correct spelling. I recall when I was in grade school, one of the best exercises I enjoyed the most was to use a dictionary in order for correct spelling. The teacher suggested, and I have never forgotten this, was to just open a dictionary and browse around. I encourage any students reading this manual to spend time poring over a dictionary. This is such a helpful creative endeavor that helps us clarify how to communicate and increase our vocabulary.

Our perceived fitness to communicate aids in directness and should not be an intimidator. Finding the simpler word is best for reaching the most, but I am amazed at how few people really know the definitions of the words they use, and how much learning is skipped when definitions are misapplied or not understood. This becomes apparent when listening to someone reading aloud. I was shocked to see how many people stunt their learning by glossing over mispronounced words they don't have a clear meaning of what they are reading.

So, the definitions of maneuver which apply to this technique are as follows. "1.b: To make a series of changes in direction and position for a specific purpose. 2. To manage into or out of a position or condition: manipulate a: to guide with adroitness and design b: to bring about or secure as a result of skillful management. - maneuverability, maneuverable, maneuverer."

The set up for the noodle is important. When coming to a stop nearside, the bus is as close to a straight line parallel to the traffic lane as possible, so that visibility in the driver side rear mirror is maximized. This is in the rule book, so that the front door is close to the curb, within six inches, and the rear door or doors, are also within one foot of the curb. Many times this is very hard to do due to lack of room created by double parked vehicles, or cars standing in the zone. But the good thing about nearside stops, is they are usually clear. If any car is at the nearside corner, odds are they can easily move away. The car is almost always attended, and when they see the bus coming up behind them, they move. So when the nearside zone is clear, pulling the bus up parallel to the curb, helps those passengers departing, and gives maximum rear visibility.

After boarding and alighting, and when the light turns green, or at a stop sign, the problem always becomes being let-in to traffic to proceed through the intersection. Keeping good car karma helps, by always allowing a turning oncoming car, or a car trying to pull out into traffic, the space to move, and not to block them. Even in construction squeeze play, I have found that best man wins, or me first, usually adds more delay than spacing which allows for a smoother merge.

When beginning to move from the zone, the noodle involves, not using the turn signal and abruptly turning left into the traffic lane, but rather to slowly move forward, straight ahead, in the curb lane. So, if an accident report should ever result, I would not have to check the box turning left, or using the left turn signal. Any operator soon finds activation of the turn signal when merging left, almost always has the unintended consequence of vehicles speeding up to pass left, and to block the merge. The thought of getting ahead of a billboarding vehicle outweighs the smoothness created in allowing us to move ahead without stopping.

Billboarding is a professional driver's term describing a blocked view. So by moving straight ahead, all cars can see that the bus is moving and clearing the zone and intersection. This also signals that the bus is finished with boarding, and no more delays will result in more people running to the door and stopping again.

If a car wants to race, that vehicle can easily pass the bus on the left as there is no conflict in the traffic lane. And this also helps, because now the bus is clearly, in the lead, in crossing the intersection for any secondary car, and the size of the bus usually stops any additional threats on the left. Because we are still parallel to traffic, we can see in our mirror any threat coming up from the rear. And as we get close to the far side crosswalk, we then move to the left, free and clear of any threat.

When I began to call the shots at when I could pull away, with clear visibility to my rear, and no threat on the intersection far side, I knew I had found the Zen of the noodle.

School Trip

THE SKILLS NEEDED BY TEACHERS are helpful in being a transit operator on school trips. I don't like receiving a coach from relief that has had a morning school trip where fast food wrappers and spilled drink cups litter the floor. I keep in mind the rider on her way to an important job interview, and the ice cream cone that fell in her lap from a young rider who lost control of her ice cream ball on top of the cone. Other memorable events are the completely full coffee cup that gets knocked out of hand when someone with a backpack passes by. Or the friendly town drunk who leaves the bottle open by the back seats and falls down to spray the odor of alcohol all over the back seats and floor. These are not the best first impressions one needs on the way to school or to work.

I always try to do harm reduction in cleaning the coach, first chance I get, but sometimes this is a few hours down the road. The best defense is a good offense, but I try not to be offensive in my comments to young people about taking their trash or wrappers or containers with them as they board the coach. But as getting to school is a predictable event with a predictable start time, the saving grace, if one could be so bold, is that you get the same riders at the same time and place every day, and because of this, you can predict who and when the trash dumpers board. And stopping them from boarding after reminding them the previous day to take their trash, shuts down much of the mess later in the week, and can have a beneficial effect on keeping the floor clean.

There is nothing like being in the Zen zone with a bunch of students going to school, and walking down the aisle after everyone has left at the terminal, and finding not one piece of dipping sauce, not one egg sandwich wrapper, and not one coffee cup by the back seats. "You're an awesome bus driver." never hurts either.

Sit Back and Watch the Show

WHEN I GET INTO TROUBLE, it becomes difficult to know what action to take, especially if I am in a rush. Paradoxically, it is when I am in a compromise, that my choice needs to be decisive and clear. If I am not in a good space, I am apt to be in "an accident." This is no more clearer than when operating large machinery with lots of souls on board. A car tries to overtake on the left, or cuts in front from the right to make a right turn at a congested intersection. This one ideal, to watch the show, allows me to avoid the need to "back up." Meditation on a regular basis about my "show" in life, has helped me immensely in knowing I am ready to make a choice. I now try to avoid blocking any vehicle in the zone by slowing, and see if the extra time cushion works. Nine times out of ten, it does.

Experience in driving a bus has given me intuition that can also arise if I take quiet time before my day opens, and when I get ready for bed at night. The patterns of my daily journey on the road become predictable, so when I see something out of place, I immediately adjust so as to keep a space cushion around the impending threat. When I was new, I would charge ahead of a taxi picking up or dropping off in the zone, but I have since realized by pacing myself to the pull-in to the curb, the taxi customer usually alights or departs, and the taxi has room to move away, thus giving me full access to the zone. I also find it easier to find a cab when I am going home from work!

Then there is the key for me to be sparing on the horn. And sure enough, I rarely need to use it now. And when I do, I try to keep it to a friendly toot and not a ship-to-ship foghorn! Blaring does nothing for keeping my serenity, and I usually get a blast back later in the day, as the equation always needs to remain balanced. I would get awful angry horns when my tail end blocked an intersection because I had rushed ahead into the zone behind another coach. I became aware of the frequency of the angry horn directed at me, and I looked at my part leading up to the situation. I also recalled the last time I gave an angry blast at another vehicle, and the hostile energy seemed to be about the same in intensity and force.

So I stopped using the horn and got light on the power pedal. And sure enough, the longer the time passed with me not using the horn, the fewer horns I got. And I started applying this invisible karmic ledger to other behaviors I found offensive to me on the road. When shocked about a car cutting me off, or a drive-by that seemed scary, I tried to recall when I made an action not anticipated by pedestrians or motorists, who may have been given the same feeling by me. And my compromising situations decreased dramatically. The suggestion to "sit back and watch the show," started to be a working part of my mind, and I got it.

Thank you for Riding!

OR SO WENT THE ANNOUNCEMENT we could cue up with our DVAS (Digital Voice Activated System.) But under new management, with the service cuts to our riders, this manually activated announcement was removed. Does this mean thanks are no longer needed? Ha ha. Just kidding. Sometimes I do get in trouble for ad-libbing on the PA or mic. Very few coaches have a clean and clear PA's, and when I have a good one, it helps when the coach is crowded. When I have been a passenger on a crowded coach, and standing in the aisle, it's very hard to see where the coach is, especially at night. I have learned from riding Muni, that calling out the stops helps people get ready to get to the door.

Timing is everything, as they say. If there is construction ahead, or a bus zone is blocked by a big truck, it is nice to open the doors nearside and let them know they can get off here. And make sure it is safe; no bikes or skaters are coming up from the rear. The mic really comes in handy when I am pulling in or going out of service. I sometimes don't have to repeat myself when everyone is in the know. I have also found that if I am willing to pop the brake and step out of the cockpit and face "the audience," I get a much more positive response in clearing the coach. I always have to mindful of my tone of voice. If I end the sentence on an upbeat note, and not an annoyed or aggravated tone, this does wonders. I am always amazed at how quickly I forget the impression I am making by how I sound. My overhead voice can go south real quick if I am impatient or feel entitled about why I think they should know my bus is going out of service. But a smile and a transfer at the box is usually all it takes.

Adding some messages under the safety cue might help, such as in the rain: "Thanks for shaking the water off your umbrella before boarding!" Some of these newer umbrellas are huge and carry lots of water! The extra water on board makes for a slippery step, and creates a jungle-like humidity in the bus which fogs up the windows. The key to keeping the windows clear, especially the front windscreen, is to hold the doors open as long as possible. This lets in the fresh air and prevents the humidity from going up too high.

When I am standing at a long red light, I keep the rear doors open, and this keeps the fresh air circulating. No one likes a puddle on their seat, so all of the side windows are closed. Also the ceiling vents have been known to create a puddle on the floor if they were left open the night before, or while in service. I always try to secure the hatches and windows if I am pulling out in the rain. Holding the doors open as long as possible keeps the air fresh and keeps my mirrors clear from fogging up. There is nothing worse than closed windows and high humidity from all the umbrellas and jackets that are wet. Keeping visibility at a max is mastered when the rear doors are held open and the baby heat settings are set for both the coach climate and the driver climate. I recently did a coach trade in the monsoon season, and had fog everywhere. But by holding open the doors, and adjusting the heat down, after just a few stops, the windows cleared.

Holding the doors open and keeping the heat to the low settings, was a gift from an old timer who had clear windows. I was at the terminal and noticed his windows were clear. His rear doors were open even though it was raining and we were at the end of the line. He came to my door and I complained I couldn't see my mirrors. "Does your bus have a better defroster?" I asked. And it was then when he explained on how he kept his windows clear: baby heat in front and back, and leave the doors open at the terminal and long red lights. I have never had to get out some newspaper and wipe the windows since. Nice. We now return you to your Zen zone, already in progress!

All Alone

ON MISSION STREET. OLD TIMERS don't mind being all alone on Mission. As a new operator I just could not fathom this. No coach visible in front looking up from Second Street to Tenth St., or looking up from 14th to 22nd. If I didn't see my leader in front of me as I left the Ferry Plaza, I would hope for help from the 49 cutting-in at S. Van Ness, which is at 12th Street. The 49 can be a help or a curse. If the 49 has extra headway on Van Ness, then it too, is full to the aisles, and can be a drag all the way out to Ocean Ave. This makes for a very slow outbound trip to Geneva. And I still don't understand why I have had such a difficult time getting over this. That is, being packed, stacked, and racked, without help and running late.

From the tranquil interior of the superintendent's office, especially when I am in trouble, comes the directive that the skip stop rule does not apply when there are no unusual delays, and no coach one block behind with the same destination. My definition of unusual delay seems as subjective as how far I can stretch a rubber band. I have skipped stops, during certain runs on a particular sign-up, because of my fears about what happens when the coach gets loaded to capacity. Interestingly, there are no capacity limits stenciled-in on the front of the coach such as found on a tour bus. This remains a mystery. And when I get into this fear fear mode, usually with anxiety creeping into my voice and shutting the door on people, trouble is not too far away.

But oddly enough, this is why I love the Mission as opposed to Chinatown. Mission is a four-lane road, although narrower than any standard midwestern town, in San Francisco, it is a blessing because this is wider than most of our streets. Mission Street is also flat, and has fewer people driving from out of town, so most motorists are cool in that they are familiar with how to get around the buses. Cars usually stop behind our coach when we are splitting the lane, and they can see the red light. The question most people ask me about how we drive is, "Why do we drive down the middle of the street?" And the answer is: "We are taught to drive that way!" This got a lot of laughs when I do my driver doug as a stand-up routine!

Coming in contact with car doors was costing the railway thousands of dollars a month in claims, so keeping a four foot right-side clearance became mandatory. This means splitting the lane down Mission Street, which is too narrow to accommodate a bus in the right lane without putting the right side at risk from doors, skaters, and bikes. Like any experienced San Francisco driving resident, they know we will soon be out of their way when the light goes green, and we pull off to the curb to pick up at our next stop.

This familiarity makes driving on the Mission, in my opinion, fun. Motorists seldom create problems, and the way is flat and wide enough to pass obstacles. Flat is good because it saves the knees and legs when braking. Especially if the coach is heavy. But the fear I have about running late and heavy and without help in front or behind is because of what begins to happen inside the coach with the passengers. "Say excuse me." "How rude." "Ouch, you stepped on my leg, my leg is broken." "Front seats are for those with disabilities, move back." "I have a disability, bitch." Don't tell me what to do mf."

And the list goes on. Fights break out. Pickpockets flourish. The chances of going out of service increase. And I guess the wisdom of many operators is to let this happen because it saves emotional energy. I have such a deep core belief in demonstrating skill in my job I consider going out of service a failure. I believe I am not using my skills appropriately to avoid going out of service. When I get written up by a passenger for taking on the load of another bus, I also feel this emotional drain. Since my job is not that of a carpenter or builder, I cannot see my handiwork as a finished product. I cannot leave a legacy so to speak, by using superior building materials, or as such, putting in four or five nails per shingle instead of skipping nails and laying down faster.

All I can do for self satisfaction as a bus driver, is to avoid fights, going out of service, and not put a burden on the operator in the coach behind me. This is how I define my success. Unfortunately, their are no awards or praise forthcoming if I prevent a breakdown, or if I skip stops to keep the bus from overcrowding. In fact, my odds for safe driving or Operator of the Month go down. All I risk is a complaint from those who get passed up, or a complaint or accident report if a fight breaks out. And so I try to find a middle ground whereby those who get passed up don't call 3-1-1, or those in my coach have just enough room to not step over one another.

And sometimes, when all alone on Mission, this becomes too challenging to find a compromise. Because if I pass up those on the corner, and there is no bus behind me, then I believe mass transit has failed to provide adequate service. Either way, service is lacking, and all I can do is try to let the folks riding I am trying to do the best I can.

This is where a good interior PA mic really helps. If they can hear me clearly when I am passing-up a stop to exit before the light, or between two corners, so I am losing more people than I gain, all is well. Interestingly, there usually is a God space to do this. Sure enough, I can find a break in the parked cars to open all my doors and let folks exit safely. There is an emergency clause in our rulebook which says we may pull to the nearest safe place to stop. I construe this emergency stop rule to mean that if I am overcrowded, even without unusual delay, this constitutes a safety violation, and that my skip stop and pass up is my highest priority. Unusual delay becomes regular delay when equipment and operators are in short supply.

53

With the installation of the drive cams on our front window, something interesting has happened. And the training inspectors, who are of my experience level and seniority, seem to have also been giving added grace by understanding that when the coach is full, certain flexibilities exist in picking up loads, and stopping. The biggest headache I have is trying to use the kneeler or lift when the coach is full. It does not seem practical or safe to pick up a wheel chair when the aisle is full. And the coach protests at having to rise when heavy, once we have lowered the kneeler. Also the wheelchair lift can get stuck if our air is too low.

If I had pixie dust to get intending disabled passengers to understand my point of view, it would be this: Yes, I want to pick up all those needing a lift, because I like the fact everyone can make their way around our city without a car. And yes, I like to feel good about myself by helping those who are less fortunate in mobility. Please be ready to board when the coach arrives, so I can see you. Let me help you by making sure you get on first. "Thanks."

Dragging the Line

WHEN A COACH IN FRONT of me seems to be taking longer than usual to leave the zone ahead of me, I must remember the one block spacing rule and slow down also to keep a healthy space between buses. This is usually an issue on Mission Street, where multiple lines parallel each other for several miles. A 49 and 14 can share a zone because the bus stops can accommodate two coaches. It is okay if two coaches unload and load together. But if there is a third bus nearby, such as a 14R, it is important to keep spacing so that no confusion arises from intending passengers as to where to board when the third coach stops to pick up. Those who need extra time to board, need that space in time between coaches to see the line and number on the coach. And if a front door is placed at the top of the zone of the leading bus, there needs to be time to adjust to the spot where the second bus opens its front door.

In order to keep spacing even, sometimes the lead coach operator will come to the back of the bus and pull poles. This will allow the emptier bus a chance to fill up by picking up intending passengers at the next stop and even out the load between the two buses. On certain pull-outs on the 14 and 49 line, a pull-out coach may be behind its leader when they both arrive at the next terminal, such as City College on the 49. The leader coach, already in service, must make way for the newer coach that leaves the terminal first, even though they arrived behind the other coach already in service. This can happen in the morning during peak period, or in the afternoon before peak period.

The newer buses have a poles down button the operator can push to make it easy for the following coach to get around. The older coaches require lowering the poles manually. And regardless of the type of coach, poles should be cradled before any coach moves. So the drama begins when the question of who should drop their poles to pass, and when.

On the 22 at the outbound terminal by Third Street, a pull-in coach arrives after its leader may stay awhile for a recovery break. On the 30 Stockton, the same situation used to occur at Beach and Broderick. Same goes for the 41, 45 at Greenwich and Lyon. Overcoming anger in trying to get around was solved if I pulled their poles and went around. But if I locked up their retrievers in the process, or caused a problem by touching their coach, I soon found this was not a good idea, and could result in payback. No, I must be the one to go around first by dropping my poles. If the other operator was indisposed and unavailable, I could always find out later what their preferences are. In the meantime, I got to go. . .

I would get so angry when an unattended had its poles up at the terminal and I had to go around. I would also not understand why an operator would leave the bus sticking way out in the traffic lane with its poles still on the wires so that a trolley could not pass. "What the hell are you doing?" was not a good way to start communication. "Is there anything I can do to help?" definitely got me out of there a lot faster. Whether a youngster locks up the rear door by letting out the air, or a defect with the lift prevents the front door from closing, it is a simple matter to either move the bus, or ask to drop the poles. Case closed and now I am free to move. Except when I am not.

I try not to rush when I am on my pull-in trip going home. I find if I have an expectation about when I am to check out, and the time changes due to delay, I have to accept this 'nature of' my job as a driver. The end time is not always exact, and I can't leave my job such as punching out on a time clock. This is what office workers and store clerks must realize when they take a driving job. I have learned it does not pay to make plans too close to my off time. Many a drama in the break room or dispatch office has been started because of an expectation that does not match the needs of the line. I would see how unattractive someone would look in appearing to be a whining baby about not getting their way. Only until I was in the same boat and being denied a day off myself! Ouch. Oh well, the nature of the beast.

But I tell you one thing. I will never let my vacation time go to zero. Nor will I let my sick time go to zero. I have found out the hard way, that when I need a day off, and I don't have it, the ability to remain calm and professional becomes difficult. I have been told to never let them see you sweat. And running out of time off seems to be a good example. God made aspirin for a reason!

Loading Zone

IN THE EBB AND FLOW of traffic, the space cushion between vehicles goes up and down. As traffic turns from medium to heavy, the matter of inches can come into play as to whether traffic comes to a standstill or not. When a limo or ride share is picking up or the motorist leaves the vehicle unattended for just the few seconds it takes to get to an ATM or get a coffee, the attitude of the car and its distance from the curb can determine if the lane is shut down and blocked. This then creates an abrupt left merge situation to lane two, and brings both lanes to gridlock. This setup for a backup is completely avoidable if the first parked vehicle would stay within 6 to 8 inches of the curb.

The pecking order of when and how delivery trucks set up to offload, also affects lane closure and gridlock. The first arriving number one truck may park in perfect order, but a second truck parks too close on the opposing traffic lane and makes for intense squeeze play that need not be if a longer gap is left open. Intending through vehicles build a backup line which prevents the oncoming lane from clearing truck one, thus preventing two way traffic from clearing. This occurs in a commercial zone where lots of cafes and shops line the street. Upper Haight in the Haight Ashbury and 18th Street between Delores and Guerrero are classic jam spots for the 33 Ashbury.

Once a delivery driver becomes familiar with his or her drop off route, adjustments are made to the delivery schedule whereby no two vehicles create a rolling delay because they wait for the other delivery to clear, and go around the block to alter their drop off time. Experienced UPS and FedX drivers are good at this. Mainly because they have another address close by and can adjust. Trash trucks can also go around the block and work on other houses or businesses if other trucks block their trash can pickup. This usually works for smaller bakery trucks and bobtails. But fifty-three foot out-of-town tractor trailers from distribution hubs in the Central Valley can cause longer line delays.

The one line delay that can block both lanes in either direction is a loading dock zone. Fifty-three foot tractor trailer rigs attempt to back into a dock perpendicular to a not-so-wide San Francisco street. These trailers take finesse and skill from the class A truck operator to make a pass in three moves maximum, else the blocked pedestrian, cycle, and vehicle traffic begin unsafe maneuvers. Office Max on Arguello near Geary, Big Lots on Mission near 30th, and the Whole Foods on 17th at Kansas are to name just a few. This just adds more delay to those patiently waiting in their lane. I have to pop the brake and relax and pretend I am watching a truck driver training video on how to back into a loading dock.

Sixty foot trolleys are being added to the 5 Fulton line and it will be interesting to see how this works on Central Avenue by the Fulton Market grocery store. A loading dock was placed on a small residential street with a trolley turn located on both corners, either side of complex which takes up the whole block. Full-length tractor trailers attempt to back in the dock whereby a space in parked cars is needed to access the dock by placing the tractor on the opposing curb to make the back-in.

The solution to this is to paint a red curb clear on either side of two residential driveways across from the dock. This means taking away parking space. Here's the rub. Taking away parking requires a procedure that takes a long time. I cannot fathom why transit needs do not gain priority over the car. Especially in a city like San Francisco. A truck making delivery to a grocery store can block commuters on the bus for up to six minutes because they can't back in to the dock because of a parked car across the street. Our event marker button on camera may help by taking a screenshot of the offending vehicle.

At the 45 terminal at Greenwich and Lyon, the red zone curb clear needed for the buses to wait their time to go downtown is not placed correctly on the block. Room for two more buses would solve the problem of coaches blocking driveways on the approach to the terminal. There are no houses on the terminal side, yet permission to move the red zone takes years to change. I hope the value of transit can be seen by all as we move into the next generation of travel. I can't understand why the planning department cannot use the eminent domain and public good to make the necessary changes for transit.

The battle cry goes up along Chestnut Avenue when bus zones need to be extended for longer trolleys. Everyone loves the fact that new larger equipment is to be added for service, but no one wants to sacrifice the three parking spaces necessary to increase the curb red zone. These delays add confusion to our General Sign Up and cause some operators to have to pull out from an alien division or extend a pull-out route from farther away from where our barn is or where we end our day.

The finale of long trailers in San Francisco occurs when a tractor trailer driver from out of town decides to go up 17th Street from Market to access Cole Valley, or takes Leavenworth from the Tenderloin to access 101 North over the Golden Gate Bridge. The loading stanchions for hooking and unhooking below the trailer scrap on the dramatic elevation change before or after crossing a steep grade. The trucks stall going uphill, or get wedged going downhill.

This recently happened when a truck got stuck crossing Union to go down Russian Hill. The only way to break free is to drag the tractor down the hill. The noise of the trailer's hitching posts dragging on the street definitely awakens anyone in a three block radius! No alarm clock needed on this commute! Tour buses are also big offenders on Russian Hill.

During Super Bowl 50, a beer truck got stuck on Jones and California by Grace Cathedral. Obviously this was a new driver on call for the extra work for the large visitor population we had hosting the Super Bowl. Tractor trailers at least have flexibility at the hitch joint. Buses are one solid mass and damage to the frame may result. I'd hate to be in their dispatcher's office when this call comes in!

Also telling are when a new fleet of delivery trucks make to the streets. New employees are easy to spot by where and when they park. They don't adapt their stop so as to not block traffic in the opposing lane. Cars waiting for a light to change block oncoming traffic trying to pass the double-parked delivery truck.

Passengers intending to board at a bus stop would also do well to adjust where they stand based on double parked vehicles nearby or next to the stop zone. While you may be standing where the bus usually stops, if other cars stand or stop in the zone or double park at the top of the key in front of the zone, this alters where we put our front door. We make a flag stop: we don't try to come to the curb. We keep our coach parallel to the curb but away from the curb lane. Usually we make a flag stop: we don't try to come to the curb and keep our coach parallel to the curb one lane away.

The simplest rule to keep the Zen is to leave a broad birth for smaller vehicles unable to see ahead, a space to move in front of my coach when they impatiently pass. I try to move to the right as much as possible so they can see the obstacle ahead, but many times this is unsafe for door openers and bicyclists. Even when passing a double parked truck, with my high beams flashing, oncoming motorists appear oblivious to my move and block me from returning to my lane. I remember I am the paid professional on the clock and a *no worries* attitude heals the block the fastest! I can find my Zen at any loading dock or any hill!

Surrender

THE MOST CHALLENGING ASPECT OF any operator of large equipment on the road is keeping aware of the "what if" possibilities. "What if" that bus in front of me, stopped in the zone, goes out of service? Did I leave enough space between my coach and the stopped coach to get around, if that bus breaks down or has a fight on board? A big no-no in the operation of a bus is to never back up. In life, of course, if we make a decision that appears to lead to an unforgiving situation, the challenge arises to decide to continue on ahead, or backtrack. The bigger the decision, the harder it is to surrender to the humility we need to go back. So too with larger vehicles, comes the fact that getting into a jam is more difficult to escape once we become boxed-in.

And so the joy of driving a small zip car becomes clear in congested situations. The fluidity smaller cars have in traffic is almost a given. That being said, my most embarrassing moments come when my bus is stuck in an intersection or my tail is blocking the crosswalk after the signal has changed to green for the crosswalk and cross street. Usually, I scan the sidewalk ahead to see who is waiting, and based on previous stops on how the leading coach departs, I make the choice to pull in to the zone behind another coach with the probability that even if my tail blocks the corner by a bit, we can usually clear the zone space before the light changes.

The contradiction of my error becomes glaring and in the form of the horn from cross traffic which cannot turn right behind me when I have stopped right behind the coach in front, and we aren't moving and the light changes, and to my horror, I see pedestrians leaving the crosswalk to walk behind my tail into the intersection space needed by a turning car to pass behind me from a turn. And this resulting rear sideswipe contact is one of the most common to buses.

In a way, pedestrians become friends in that their walk space puts an added cushion on my rear. But when pedestrians don't cross, usually because a car is aggressively pulling forward to turn, is when the danger zone becomes active. Not knowing the mood or state of the cross traffic when the light does change, is a blind spot that can and often does, lead to trouble. Even when a car decides to cross over the center line to pass me while I am stopped at a green, any collision they get into is not on me. I see no merit in creating more paperwork.

And so too with life, if things are moving fast and we feel light and free, we rarely stop to think about any negative consequences arising from having to know a 'what if.' But if we are doubtful about our next move, and we feel heavy and distressed, I have come to believe not to decide is to decide: not to move ahead even if the light is green. I have a problem with understanding this.

Not to decide is to decide. What the hell does this mean? It has always struck me as being like a cop-out. And this is where being behind the wheel of a bus has helped me in my life in other decisions where I could not guess the outcome. Which is to wait until the way is clear. My codependence about what others' think in the immediate, i.e. the car behind me honking to push me through the green, has pushed me to move ahead behind the other coach. But as like attracts like, my move forward comes with even more anger with the honk from the car trying to turn behind me after the light changes.

This paradox took me a long time to be able to integrate in all areas of my life. That when running late and running heavy, the impulse to move up, or to push the envelope and try to cut down on waiting time, very rarely pays off. My co-workers and trainers would mention this time and time again as a precursor to an accident, and only when I have seen this over a long period of time, did I finally get the message. Usually when I am in the lead, and another coach moves in too close to me, do I realize how uncomfortable I feel. I immediately have to forgive myself because I have done the same thing myself. Rather than get angry at my follower, I can kill a stale green and cross on the amber nearside at the next stop to indicate I don't want him or her to follow me far side.

When I was a rookie, and a senior operator was coming up close behind, the best thing I could do would be to pull my poles and get out of their way. They usually smiled and moved on up ahead. The most frustrating thing about all of this is when they tailgate, but they don't want to move out in front. I have to muster all the courage and serenity I have to not let them affect my driving and decision making. I did learn early on, that seeing the rear end of the bus in front of me is not a happy day. And being a free range chicken is much easier than having a train of trolleys in front, or worse, in front and in back.

This becomes the most challenging aspect of not "winning" the race--when there are too many buses bunched together. The master of this principle will immediately adjust her speed and time in the zone by leaving the door open and pausing before moving forward, keeping the one block spacing rule in mind. And this rule is the clearest for me to see. The one block spacing rule is the best rule for avoiding an avoidable accident.

I tend to be too much an all or nothing guy, with little head space for a steady, easy course. Pacing myself in all my comings and goings has been a lifelong challenge I did not relate to this rule.

By doing several small steps in a series of activities, such as writing this chapter now, then going to the store for groceries, and then having a stretch and a snack, creates a world I would not uncover once I get into the hour-by-hour zone of being stuck doing one thing. Same is true with obsessing about something in my mind. I did not see how the idea of surrender was actually what I was doing by pacing myself in doing a term paper, studying for a test, or working out in the gym. My sleepless cramming for a test, a torn rotator or tennis elbow, pigging-out at a breakfast bar, were all the endgame chargeable "accidents" resulting from a pattern of not surrendering. But I can say, if I find myself having to back away from a coach dead in the water, I can immediately choose to take a point of gratitude in seeing where I went wrong to not make the same mistake again.

I can eat a snack before a large meal. I can stretch before I hit the weights, I can use flash cards or reread my class notes later in the same day to burn the information in rather than do nothing and then try to cram. So surrender can actually means pacing myself based on what others are also doing. It keeps resentment at bay.

No better a traffic example is on I-5 between S.F. and L.A. Or in inner city medium traffic during off peak hours when everyone is cruising at about the same speed and distance. Stress is low and everyone is content with making the same time. I also had to learn this lesson about how the CHP also handles traffic. If everyone is doing 70, and there are no obstacles such as weather or construction, they tend to let "free-range traffic' to continue uninterrupted at pace. Like an idiot, when I was new to California from the midwest, cruising with everyone at 75, I did panic when I saw an oncoming cruiser, and brake abruptly to slow to 60. All I did was call attention to myself, and he immediately began braking to look for a safe crossover. Luckily, there was none, and only later at a big truck stop did I find the unwritten California traffic rule of live and let live, as long as no one is causing problems contrary to the flow, let it go. So I guess another form of surrendering is to blend into what the flow or trend is telling you.

Headway

"WHEN IS THE NEXT BUS coming?" "Is there another bus behind you?" "How long before you go?" All of these questions are actually about headway. Headway is the time in minutes between buses. People usually ask me what is the best line to drive. And I say to you now the real question is, "What line has the best headway when I am scheduled to work?" Which follows to the important question, "What line has a headway where the loss of a leader allows for enough time to have a break at the terminal?" Or, when I won't "get killed," or "hit" with an impossible passenger load? Loss of a leader means the bus in front of me is not in service or not out.

A "not out" is a radio term for letting the following operator know they don't have a leader. And I have found the 24 Line and 49 can be okay to work without a leader most weekday mornings. Some would argue the 6 line is okay without a leader, but I have not found this to always be the case. A lot depends on who is working the bus in front of me.

And the term "working" carries with it a loaded gun meaning, because not all operators seem to be working when they sit behind the seat. So having a non-working leader with a not out in front of me can make for a challenging 4 hour period without a break. And I have found if I go more than four hours without a working leader with double headway, I at some point, leave the Zen zone. And I need to be aware of the warning signs that I am beginning to break down emotionally. I am now good enough where I can outrun or outpace the equipment. A bad bus with low air or slow doors can make matters worse, but I have enough body energy to overcome most defects. It just is a matter of time before I begin to leave the Zen zone and start to risk angry passengers or unprofessional conduct. Some times the transit Gods step in and the bus complains and groans to a stop. Time out for calling the shop.

When I was new, I had trouble in ignoring the defects the coach was signaling to me, and kept going instead of taking a time out for myself. This subjective call differs from person to person, and I have had to do a lot of work on myself to see I cannot make the call about someone else's personal break down point, or judge whether or not I thought they should or could keep going in service.

I recently had slow doors and doors that would not close all the time. I was dragging down the line. I was heavy, and too many people were waiting at the next zone. I began to pass up. The key is to know when to start picking up again. Sometimes I overdo the pass-up and get a "love letter" from the superintendent. I turned the corner on to Otis by 12th and passed up about eight people. Though I did have room for them, there was another bus behind me. But this time they didn't see it, or weren't in the mood to wait. Whoops. I can feel it right away. The rule is to stop and ask them to take the next coach, but my Zen was gone from having "made it" past busy Van Ness. I made a mistake, and sure enough, pen went to paper to result in a confer and consult with my union rep and superintendent. But I do find myself more relaxed than in the past. I am only human. My coach had defects which I chose to take me out of the Zen zone instead of slowing down and asking for help. Minding my own business was all I needed to 'worry' about.

Being a victim never works.

Getting along with my co-workers was perhaps the last feather in my cap. Accepting I could not make the call on someone else's coach or how they operate, was the first step in not getting mad about someone or something outside of my control, and put me in the Zen zone I so admired from senior operators who never seemed to be phased with what was going on in the bus in front of them.

When I was asked by another more senior operator about how many buses I was driving, I didn't get what she was asking. But I get it now. I only have one bus to operate, and that minding my own business was all I needed to take care of. Trying to do too much usually got me into the superintendent's office, or to sign for "love letters" at the dispatch desk from a passenger complaint. I knew I was on a good track when these events stopped happening to me! The only mail I get now is a Christmas card from the superintendent in December. This is mail I like to get! Merry Christmas!

So the feeling I was owed more time gradually became less and less important, and the statement from senior operators who I only have one bus to drive finally came home. And as the years have passed, I see it matters less and less what others do or don't do. What is important is what I do. Work the rule, and call for help if I need it.

The guessing game about which run and line has a reasonable headway has become less of a hard homework problem, and more about just leaving on time and doing what Central Control always assures us to do when we call in late and heavy: to do the best we can.

Packed Stacked and Racked

ALLITERATION ASIDE, I LOVE THIS phrase when describing a bus which simply cannot take on one more passenger. One would think when the bus becomes completely grid locked on the inside aisle, common sense by simple observation would be enough to insure no one intending at the bus zone would consider even getting on the bus. One would be wrong if one thought that. In fact, there probably is a correlation coefficient that as the number of people waiting for the bus increases, their willingness to look inside the coach and see if there is room for boarding, decreases.

And this pile-on and pile-in to effect is some thing I always hope to avoid. And I can, but it means I have to pass up stops to keep from becoming so full I can't see past the yellow line. I can get all sorts of help from passengers who want to "help out" by hearing them yell at the group to move back or to make room for a seat for a senior, but their "help" sometimes creates more problems because of the tone of their voice, or the profanity they may use. It is at this time I feel as though I am losing control of the situation. And the hard part is to figure out when it is time to stop taking on more people.

This is not as simple as it would first sound, because one has to figure on how many people are getting off. It is a simple math equation performed at every stop or transfer. How many did I lose and how many am I picking up? Through intuition and experience, it does become easy to know if I am going to lose more than I gain, but there are some whoops moments. I have room for six, but there are ten waiting. If I know I usually lose four or five, I should be okay and make the stop. But uh oh, here come five people running, only one person gets off, and now the light goes red and here comes a walker and a person with shopping bags. Should I have passed up the preceding stop to allow for this margin of error? Should I make the announcement that this coach is full, and will they listen to me? And this is where the ninth level of hell begins. But what I can do is shut this trend down immediately by passing up the next stop,

The danger is you don't want people waiting at the stop to see there is room in the back, even if for a few. But once again, some equipment cannot maintain full capacity for more than two hours, and this other factor is hidden from view. Also the number of people waiting at the next transfer point is also not clear to intending pass-up passengers. So the idea here is to pass up when the coach is full, but in a way the minimizes drama and coach failure. And it is this see saw that makes life interesting. I have to approach this the way I approach spider solitaire: through difficult moves can come sweet victory.

Split Doors Split Groups

Sometimes, when the bus is very crowded, and there are a large number of people waiting on a busy corridor, people get stuck on the front steps. If a group of people are only "half on" the bus, some in the party go to the back door. But if the front door clears first, and the back doors shut, the bus takes off, and those who ran to the back door don't get on. Many times our rear mirror visibility is blocked if someone is moving to the rear on the sidewalk just outside of our narrow curb view. And this results in a split group. Usually the party on the bus near the front door, demands to get off immediately. This may not be safe or possible after having pulled into heavy traffic, such as on Van Ness which is highway 101 from Mission to Lombard. Under these conditions it is difficult for me as an operator to determine who is in what party, and if I have cut a group in half. Having been familiar with the 30 Stockton in Chinatown, I look for a break in the bodies, so I can close the doors without hitting anyone.

The key is to size up the group in approach, and to stop the bus and doors proximate to where the intending group is standing. If I have more room in the back, I can stop slightly forward of the mass, encouraging the group to enter in the rear. By clicking open all rear doors, most folks tag in on the rear door taggers, and I see those with fast passes flashing me as they board in the rear. The decals on the door to enter in the front do give tourists pause, and they migrate to the front door. Or the person paying the fare decides to come to the front door as the others in their party enter in the rear. I need to accept that those with cash fare in their hands, may not come to the front door. I choose to accept the fact I cannot see everyone's

71

fare, and to consider the paying of the fare as an honor system. I am emotionally much more relaxed to do a better job and pay attention to safety.

This is why some become displeased when it appears we are not doing our job by collecting fare. We are paying attention to our highest priority, rather than spend the emotional turmoil of taking fare evasion as a personal affront. This is not always unavoidable. Sometimes a person who has the cash to pay the fare tries to come to the front door, and they are blocked by people standing on the steps. The rear doors close when I see the sidewalk has cleared, and the fare payer gets left on the curb.

It also gets interesting when the luggage of the tourist, fresh off of BART from the airport, gets separated during the split doors, split groups situation. The best way to avoid this is to keep together and wait for the next bus. If buses have been passing by completely full, panic or impatience sets in, and bad choices start to rise and contribute to getting lost in the shuffle. A stop such as Kearny/Geary/ Market is such a stop. Tourists need answers to questions about where I go, but this is not a good time and place to get into twenty questions. Especially when other buses are behind me, and a new group from the N Judah underground are running to my now full coach.

If I can get past Kearny and Market without a problem, I know I am in the Zen zone of driving a bus.

Pulling Poles

WHEN A COACH BECOMES DISABLED after an accident or a security incident, if the operator is occupied with the police or an inspector, it is important they are not blocking traffic or other trolleys coming up from behind.

It is embarrassing to me when a transit bus appears to be the problem in causing a traffic delay. Practicing defensive driving, if practiced on a daily basis, almost down to the minute-to-minute decision making choices we make on the road, can make the difference between smooth flowing traffic and gridlock.

The experience from the inspector called to a post-accident scene also provides valuable lessons about how to keep my side of the street clear. Since inspectors meet with operators time and time again, post accident, their directness about getting to point quickly is an art I have always admired. And when their report matches my description, I know I have taken a valuable lesson with me.

If I am coming up from behind, I have learned being of service not only means keeping my passengers informed, but I can pop the brake and help another operator who is blocked or out of service. But pulling poles is an opportunity to respect boundaries and to check-in with the other operator to find out if they need my help.

And I see this principle in many situations. If a senior appears to be having difficulty in getting up the steps, it is also important to ask them first if they need help. Sometimes, no help is desired, and by touching them without permission, bad feelings result. I want to be left alone, or I do not need any help because I am able, are two big reasons why seniors don't desire assistance, and it is hard to know this simply by looking at their climb up the steps. Most times, though, if I see a heavy load, all my angst melts away when I offer to help. And so it is also true if another bus is blocking with the poles up on the wires and not moving, I must first ask, "Do they need my help?" The next question, which is usually my first question when I am in the swerve, is where the hell are they? If the operator has gone to the store, or gone the bathroom, then I can pull their poles and go around without having to drop mine. The time cuts on the 49, when severe, make for a tight terminal situation, and getting around can sometimes be a drag. If I arrive on my leaving time, and I desire another nice trip without overcrowding, I can zip by my leader and go. But my attitude really checks what kind of day I have when it comes to pulling poles.

Some operators, using the rear view mirrors as directed, see me coming and drop their poles by using the poles down button, or coming to the rear of their coach and cradling them. Others expect to not be bothered, and if I want to avoid stink eye and a nasty vibe, it is up to me to get around, even if I don't have a poles down button. If at a terminal with more than one track, such as North Point, I scan across the way to see if the operator is present in the coach. If not, I can stay on the left track and bypass without any hassle. This is the one saving grace at terminals with two sets of wires (the 22 Fillmore and 24 Divisadero at Third Street could use this extra set of wires) But throw in tourists in rental cars holding the famous freebee Fisherman's Wharf map, and a backlog of 30 Stockton coaches which share the terminal, and all bets are off!

One of the biggest, nastiest paybacks is when the number one coach is waiting its time at the terminal when you are the follower and ready to pull-in. Add some rain or wind, and passengers who have been waiting twenty minutes for a bus, and the decision to wait it out and pull-in late becomes the better option. Oh well, so much for that meeting or movie or dinner after work. Even if no payback situation exists, there is nothing worse than seeing on the first day of a new sign-up, who your leader is, at your final pull-in terminal. This can either be icing on the cake (they pull their poles) or one more straw on the camel's back. Of course, usually by the time you get to your last terminal, you already know what kind of a leader you have! Which is another way of saying, who is doing the work?

Getting to the respect of my co-workers was one of the hardest and longest lessons I needed to get at work. The traffic, the passengers, and the equipment were no longer a problem. Even the angry addict at 16th and Mission pulling poles to steal my transfers while I walked back to put up the poles, were no longer a deal. It was getting right with my coworkers who took the longest time to find my Zen. The only way this can happen is if I love myself.

Secure the Coach

PART OF TESTING A NEW operator in being qualified by a state inspector is coach securement. As this book is written by a trolley operator, the added requirement of coach securement is in cradling the poles by the hooks near the harp at the back of the coach. Many a day goes by where a coach is taken out of service on the line and the operator fails to secure the coach in a timely fashion. Of course, there could be a lot of argument about what qualifies as timely fashion, but the bottom line is no coach can stay on the wires from behind an unsecured trolley with its poles still on the overhead wires.

Hell No! When my leader goes out of service with a full coach on my time, I am glad I remember the one block spacing rule and not get too close. I can drop my poles and go around. Nothing worse than double headway and a full load. Hell no! means I am not going to continue for the rest of the trip with angry intending passengers waiting at the curb and have a full bus with no room. Hell no! means I can pass by the coach and continue on to the next stop without missing a beat. My follower can take all of his people, and I can pick up all of my leader's people still waiting at the next bus stops. This causes minimal disruption to the line and keeps buses spaced properly.

This is against the rules which state pass ups are only after an unusual delay and another bus with the same destination is one block behind. I will roll past an out of service bus as an unusual delay, and pass up those passengers so I don't drag down the line and make the gap even bigger. This is a violation of the letter of the law, but the letters don't account for the emotional tension that comes on board a few stops later when I am full and cannot pick up. I choose the path of least resistance.

Show how its done. When there is no bus behind me I have an obligation to pick up those stranded by the bus that went out of service. It is these times I get my swerve on and take care of business. As long as I have no one in front of me, I have a clear shot to move up and put an end to the dragging coach. As I don't work with my hands like a construction worker, it is harder to get a sense of satisfaction in seeing a finished project. The day is a great one if I can get to a terminal before my leaving time: Just a 'thank you' as the last person departs! Just the hope of a thank you from the last passenger getting off at the end of the line. "Step down here for a great walk along the waterfront of Aquatic Park and check out the swimmers in the bay. Alcatraz views are plenty so make sure your camera is handy. Ghirardelli hot fudge sundaes are also only two blocks away!" These statements of gratitude are the only 'things' I get to 'make.'

If and when we get help with the shop, or an inspector is called to the scene, there actually is a friendly pat on the back!. The shop or inspector taps our rear below the last window to let us know our poles are placed back on the wires and we are clear to use the power pedal and continue on our way on the wires. "Nice day."

Knowing the Lights

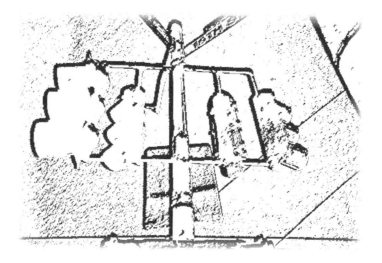

JUST LOOKING AT THIS CHAPTER heading, it sounds spiritual. And indeed, the effect of using knowledge and experience about when traffic lights turn green feels spiritual. It feels like going with the flow. When I time the lights and bring the coach slowly up to the stop line, and the light goes green, it saves wear and tear on my knees and on the coach brakes. But very few motorists take advantage of this idea. Time after time, cars whizz by my coach only to be stopped at the next block, waiting for the light to turn. Here I come, lumbering up to the intersection, only to roll past them with my momentum coasting me to the other side before they put the pedal to the metal. The amount of money and energy that could be saved if even 20 percent more motorists approached stale reds at an even pace, is probably a huge number when the multiplier effect is considered. Because I, as a transit operator, go through intersections up to eight times a day, at least five days a week, I get the knowing about when I can make a light, or when speeding up pays no dividends. Motorists, who may be randomly taking a trip choice not made on a regular basis, don't necessarily know the lights. And this does cause delay. Particularly when turns are involved.

And the lights are not the same throughout the day. In the morning, greens I can make, become impossible in the afternoon. Timing of the lights also changes. But once the timing is figured out, all the guesswork is removed, and the job becomes relaxing and easy. I had so much anxiety when I was new, because I didn't know the lights, and I could not tell if it was safe to cross over the line as the light turned red. It is impossible for vehicles to cross our intersections here in San Francisco with three second yellows. No way can a sixty foot coach clear an intersection with only a three second amber. But in knowing the flow, all this becomes academic.

It is also important to see how the intersection flows with the cross traffic. Is the street one-way? Does the direction of cross traffic travel enhance crossing late, or does it hinder? Is cross traffic turning or is it mostly flowing straight? Every intersection is different due to pedestrian and car volume, and most problems are caused by motorists and pedestrians not familiar with the flow.

When I already know if I can or cannot clear an intersection, my day becomes easy. Simply by counting the number of people waiting at a stop, I already know before I pick up, whether or not I can make the light before it turns red. And I can also know the point of no return when it comes to approaching traffic coming up from the rear. If I can pull away from the curb before the next group of cars arrives, I am good to go.

But I do make errors when cars get too close, and I have to surrender. The hardest part for me to accept is that of surrender. I don't have to win. And I always have to check my spiritual condition to make sure I am in surrender, and not in "win" mode. When I stay in win mode, I am actually in loser mode. And if I see a threat approaching, I have to check myself and get back to surrender. If a car is approaching faster than other vehicles, I must immediately surrender to that vehicle. If a car wants to "win" to get to the intersection first, I must take my foot off of the power pedal and let them win. And when I lumber up behind them when they are stopped at the next red, I always leave extra space. And I always try to let them have complete visibility. I stop back so they can see if it is safe to turn, or if someone is stepping off of the curb late.

Limited sight distance is one of the biggest hazards living in a dense city where the buildings come up close to the sidewalk. By stopping back behind the line, most of my problems have gone away. Knowing the lights reduces hard braking and trespass upon the crosswalk. Knowing the lights is a good metaphor for life in general. If we are new to a task or assignment, it helps to get feedback by watching those with more experience and to learn from our observations of their actions. So, for me, knowing the lights is actually a form of surrender of not being first.

The final aspect of surrender that took me longest to accept is when a car passes on the right when I am preparing to make a right turn. If a car tries to squeeze in on the right, I have to adjust my stopping point. So the biggest offense is the best defense. And this keeps me in the Zen zone.

Car Karma

I RECENTLY RENTED A CAR share to go downtown to buy some bins for my storage closet and screens for my windows. When I say I am not a car person, I mean it. This becomes painfully clear when I try to park around downtown in a car. I am much more comfortable in a bus than in a car.

My friends ask in awe about how I can manuever such a large vehicle in traffic, but being bigger has it's advantages. I have much clearer visibility up high with lots of big mirrors. In a car, I am more or less an equal, and I am continually shocked at how close people tailgate and fail to leave a space cushion around me. The lack of using turn signals is perhaps the biggest failure of motorists, and they seem oblivious to how the simple act of signaling your intention can prevent gridlock and reduce conflict and collision.

It can be seen that the reason a turn signal is not given is because the driver does not know where they are going! Seeing a back seat driver or a passenger with a map open is telling. Large car share stencils over the paint job of an auto alert regular city drivers that a novice is behind the wheel, and to give wide berth!

Wide berth, however, is inexcusable with your car's ass sticking out more than 18 inches from the curb! The thought *I am only going to take a second* is no reason to park more than a foot away from the curb, or to double park. Especially on two-way streets. The red curb is red for a reason. We need the curb space to clear a turn.

On the bus I have what I call photon torpedoes. I can mark a spot on the ongoing video in front of my bus to capture a license plate of an offending vehicle blocking the transit lane or bus zone. I feel smugly complacent in generating revenue for the city at the flick of a switch, until I take away the notion of being separate from the people I was photographing. Being in a car share to pick up some office storage bins had me worried about my car karma. I had big stencils on my car and would be tagged as an idiot from the start. Would I end up being the same inconsiderate driver when loading bins into the hatchback?

I parked in the 5th and Mission garage and decided to carry the bins to the car in the garage. The store wouldn't let me use a dolly to roll to the garage one block away. No problem, I thought, I can carry them. They were light but bulky. When I got to the the garage, the top bin caught on an overhead exit sign and the whole load tumbled to the floor, cracking the lids on all of them! Perhaps this was payback for all the tickets I issued to folks going Christmas shopping one month earlier!

I have since not seen the bus with the photon torpedo cameras, and I don't take a picture of a vehicle's plates if the car is not hindering any passenger to get to my front door. Only in the case of loading a wheelchair or someone on crutches, do I make a photo record of the offending vehicle blocking the curb. I allow any car intending to pull out from a parked position space to move into the traffic lane if traffic is creating a solid wall without a gap with which to move into the flow. If someone needs to get into their car, and I am in stopped traffic, I now always give them a car space to open their door and get in. Sure enough, I am let into the passing lane when blocked from a turning car. As I allow others to merge, so am I given that Grace.

I can follow the Zen of not identifying anyone as stupid, and understand we are all trying to do the best we can with what we have been given.

Next Bus

TRANSIT TIME IS NOT LIKE real time. The digital next bus time is displayed on most bus zone shelters with the estimated time of arrival for the next two buses. But anyone who has spent any time in the bus zone knows that the arrival time displayed by next bus is not a given. Sometimes the countdown stops. Sometimes the countdown to arrival actually increases in minutes. Sometimes the sign states that the bus is arriving when no bus is is sight. And then it shows a bus departing and there is no bus. What causes these invisible arriving and departing buses? Any one of a million possibilities.

But the interesting point here is that municipal railway time is not constant. As a transit operator, we are continually making adjustments in our mind, followed by actions at the light or bus stop to continually readjust our headway, depending upon whether we are ahead or behind our regularly scheduled arrival or departure time at the various checkpoints along our line. Because sometimes leaving late is a means to an end to arrive early at our next terminal. Other times, leaving early is a huge mistake and actually causes us to arrive late at our next terminal. But how could this be?

If I leave Daly City early, I may have a large group waiting for me at the Evergreen stop which is the major transfer point from points south in San Mateo county from our sister transit agency, SamTrans. My time spent in the zone here and in subsequent stops to Geneva, the first major transfer point in the city limits, "costs" an extra five to seven minutes. Picking up seniors and those without fast passes takes extra time at the fare box, which is our biggest factor in our average miles per hour, or rate at which we move through our trip to our next terminal. Very few folks have a fast pass at Evergreen. If the 14 Rapid coach is late, or missing it's leader, the local coach, the one I am driving, can become heavy with standees, and run late. If the other helper coach, the Rapid, arrives first to Geneva, this can help when I arrive there as less people are waiting. I would then lose more people getting off to go to Balboa Park BART than would be waiting to board and go downtown. And this difference in passenger load affects comfort levels and number of seats for seniors.

So I have to make the decision to leave a little earlier to compensate for the heavy load and delay at the fare box, but this increases the chance that I will arrive first at Geneva, the first major transfer point in the city. This would keep me heavy inbound to Ocean, and delay my arrival to my inbound terminal. If I hold back and leave Daly City later, I might get help from the Rapid, and might not be as full, as this other coach would arrive at Lowell first and also maybe at Geneva, so I would start to become lighter and have less passenger congestion problems. These considerations can lead to a game of you go first, and create bigger gaps between buses. And so those waiting at Daly City are in the constant state of struggle and flux, asking the time worn phrase, "Are you the first coach to leave?"

Let the games begin. . . and why lines get eliminated. Case in point: the number 7 Haight would wait at the Golden Gate Park terminal across from the Golden Arches until the 71 Noriega would come and barrel around the corner to pick up at Stanyan and Haight. Waiting for the 71 would cause the 71 to become even heavier and run later, because the 7 wouldn't leave on time from the park terminal. And by holding back three minutes, the 7 could shadow behind the the 71. By looking at the numbers of passengers on the 7, management decided to eliminate the 7. Now the 71 has been renumbered as a 7 and the old Haight trolley is gone.

So why would not these games have a referee such as an inspector monitoring leaving times? Good question. Now that all coaches have cameras, and all coaches can be monitored by GPS on laptops, many such delays have been saved. When the Rapid coaches run in packs on the Mission, the regularity of space between coaches becomes somewhat disrupted. When I keep getting asked, "When is the Rapid coming?" It is a safe bet that they are leaving late from the Ferry so as to not run hot. But if they would just leave on time and pace properly, this question would never be asked. When a sign-up becomes stale, and the games get heavy, everyone starts hoping for a new schedule. I notice my headway and load factors improve dramatically a few weeks before the end of a sign-up. It was because leaving times and checkpoints were being observed by inspectors. How I wish I did not have to wait for the end of the signup for paperwork to be served. The difference to job quality by running on time is astonishing.

Another wait and see was at South Van Ness and Mission, where the 47 could wait at the light by Goodwill, and allow the 49 Van Ness to go first to pick up the waiting hordes at Market. If the 49 in front of these following two coaches was shadowing behind the 14 line on Mission and holding back to do less work from Ocean, it becomes clearer as to why these gaps in buses occur, and why wait time increases. This only causes operators to avoid this blob and hold back hoping that the coach from the other barn has to be first to do the "work." This gives management the incentive to eliminate runs where the following bus is usually empty.

These terminal or layover cuts have been re-instituted on the 49 line after a reroute along South Van Ness ended. Instead of taking away the four minutes we gained by not traveling along slower Mission Street, ten minutes were taken away. This makes for at least one in three coaches unable to make a full trip on time. If street operations orders one in three coaches to take Persia or Post, all is okay. But they only choose to do this once a week. It is either feast or famine on the line. Heaven help us when trying to sign up for a new work schedule. Manipulation of the money and the run time makes it challenging to pick a "safe" run when signing up for a new schedule.

So when the schedule works, and everyone leaves on time, less time is left to keep the gaps even, and terminal or recovery time is reduced. If things get busy, we don't have enough time left in our recovery time at the terminal to leave on time as we arrive after our leaving time. By being "efficient" in reducing buses that are usually empty, all hope of keeping the schedule goes away, and the gaps between late buses become more frequent

Perhaps the key becomes not to allow a long enough recovery time at the terminal so an operator can leave early.★

★some or all of the content herein does not necessarily reflect the views of the SFMTA or its policies and rules.

Nowhere in Particular

ONE OF THE HAPPIEST ZEN zone times I have experienced driving the bus is at the end of a swing shift, or the shift operators call the twilight. After completing my last full trip on the 49 Van Ness, I had a pull-in to Eleventh and Mission, so I remain in service along Van Ness outbound from North point and Aquatic Park, to Market St. We can usually put up the Market St. destination sign. But on the old trolleys, there was the sign "Nowhere In Particular." Usually, no one pays any attention to the destination sign. They only look at the line sign and board, assuming the coach will continue to its regular terminal destination. And one of the social experiments I like to try is to see if various head signs work to my favor by getting attention, or by limiting the number of questions I get asked about where I am going. Often, when I have had a long day, and I am exhausted from a heavy day, I try to see if I can pull in without delays with confusion at the front door and fare box about my short line status. Sometimes, one brief announcement is all it takes, and everyone departs willingly and knowingly without any confusion.

Other times, when I inform them at the door I am a short line coach, it creates confusion about what choice to make, and if there is another coach coming. And I sometimes can't tell in advance if I will have to expend more energy in overcoming a lack of understanding, and try to make clear over and over, one on one about my out of service stop, or whether I can keep quiet, and wait till the last stop.

Sometimes people get angry when I go out of service. The sense is I have failed them or I am not doing my job. Such as, I am intentionally stopping short and I am scamming the system and cutting-out early. I have to adjust my thinking to realize they may have had a bad experience on an earlier trip that day, or that they have been cut short by some other run or pull-in where the operator did not follow the rule of announcing the pull-in correctly or without regard for their need. And this understanding took a while to get used to. Their anger is not about me, but about some other time and place.

So one night near Halloween, on my pull in from North point, I saw the paper in the scroll roller was torn and would get caught and tear a bigger rip. So I had to look for another sign to put up that would be clear I was not going all the way out to Ocean. And, being in a playful mood, I decided to scroll all the way up to "Nowhere In Particular." And this was a good decision. I got a lot of smiles along the way. Even some toots from coaches going in the other direction. People were noticing the sign more so than if I had put up the standard sign of "Mission," or "Market." I did not have to waste any impatient energy with all those I came in contact with who were waiting at the bus stops along Van Ness. And they waited for the next bus to take them beyond my pull-in point. So I didn't have to say anything. The few who did get on were in a good mood, and obliged nicely by getting off at my last stop without a peep. "I wish I could go where you are going! Good night." Wow. What a difference from the usual groans or sighs. So my playful energy transferred perfectly, and no one complained. I was in the Zen zone on my pull in trip instead of getting stink eye or endless questions.

The biggest test of the Zen zone is on a pull in trip without incident or delay. I am sad this sign was not included in the new digital readout of the new head signs. I have always wondered who gets to make the decision to encode the destination roster, and who gets to program in the automatic announcements. I wonder what department they are in, and what other tasks they may have at their job.

Most riders believe that as an employee for the railway, we know about many details. Such as when is the next bus coming. And when I was new, I did not have much to go on. But with the bus shelters displaying the waiting time between coaches, some of the confusion has gone away. I try to look to see the next bus display in the shelter to see if I can read the next arriving time. I am always hopeful new tech can solve Muni problems. But I am sad when some of the humor and creativity is taken away as an older tech, like the paper scroll is removed. The newer LED lighting is not necessarily easier to read than the old black and white paper signs. And although the GPS technology helps customers a lot, sometimes I think adding computers or chips to buses was a dumb idea.

Oh well, "Nowhere In Particular" was a fun sign to put up, and seemed to get a good response from everyone when I used it. There are those few precious times when it seems okay to put up a more unusual sign, and it was neat to have had that option.

The Late Ring

NOTHING CAN GET A PASSENGER angrier than passing up a stop. I can tell a lot about their day by how they respond when I pass-by where they wanted to get off. Intuition does come into play when I am in the beat of the flow, and I know to stop and open the doors even if their was no ring or verbal request. We transit operators joke we don't have eyes in the back of our head or possess supernatural powers to mind read the desires of our passengers. But actually, we do have these extraordinary skills or abilities. With the experience that comes from years of driving the various lines and routes, at all different times of day and night, we do kick into an automatic pilot mode that remembers where and when to stop, and how many people will be getting off and on, but we never let on to this because ignorance, although not an excuse during a disciplinary hearing, is bliss. Contrary to the blissful ignorance we master through the years, is the expectation of need from our riders, without any verbal communication at all. This is the Zen of driving a bus.

As soon as we see something out of the ordinary, we immediately file it away in our head as a possible yellow flag. This ability to flag an abnormality to our flow, such as a distracted passenger, or the time it takes for someone to sit down, and where they sit when they first board, is a way in which we prepare for a possible mind read situation when the person is ready to get off.

And if the boarding passenger goes into the black hole, the seat behind us, where we cannot see or hear them, the risk of a pass-up or late ring goes way up. If they are in a large party and are talking among themselves, particularly tourists, then the late ring pass-up increases dramatically. How a person passes us by at the fare box is a key to understanding the drama of how they leave the coach. No eye contact or acknowledgement of our existence increases the intensity of anger they may express when they attempt to leave. No courtesy or recognition of us doing our job, and fare evasion, go hand in hand with nasty name calling at the end of this boarding event. The attention to detail when a person boards is the secret to having the magic of mind reading or eyes in the back of our head.

Some operators never use the interior center or aisle mirror located in front of us above the windscreen, but by scanning this mirror as we are directed to scan left-right-left on our exterior mirrors, passenger problems can go to near zero. Also the small mirror in the corner by the front door is perfect for aiming at the black hole. Thus I can see everyone in the seats toward the back door, and the two seats directly behind the cockpit, should someone shift their body position in anticipation of the stop. And can I get the heads up if someone is falling asleep, or inattentive to where the bus is headed. By standing up and letting a would be sleeper know this is their stop, helps prevent a lost cause at my next terminal or pull-in. If a chime cord is not working, or the dash light indicating a stop request is not lighting up, the mirrors come to the rescue of what can be a Zen breaker, usually resulting in name calling and verbal abuse.

But the danger I have in appearing unconcerned with someone who wants to get off, is that I get so complacent in knowing the rhythm of my day, I don't allow for differences in my passenger requests. If I have passed up a baby stop at a certain time week after week, my automatic pilot fails me if I haven't been scanning my rear interior mirror. And hence my Zen is broken by an angry stop request. "Back door!" is a friendly reminder of my remiss, but nasty name calling has me usually proceeding to the next stop. And the anger with which someone directs to me, the longer the next stop may be. I have to fight the demons of resentment within me to stop when someone is very angry. Anger doesn't usually work with me. I like to strike back with indifference to meet their expectation. Hey, if I am a blind idiot or a moron, than it fits I continue on to the next stop, as any faithful moron would! But if that God-given break in parked cars is available, I stop when safe to do so. It is when there is no place to safely stop that drama crescendos in a late ring. But I do recover from such name calling a lot faster now then when I was new.

And if the late ring is from someone who needs the curb, I do feel bad when I can't find a safe spot a short distance from the regular bus stop. Even though other passengers may come to my rescue by agreeing there was no ring, it has little comfort to the angry passenger. All I can do is file the incident away as another awareness point as a problem time and place, and recall where the offending passenger boarded, so as to prevent the late ring from happening again in the future. By stopping next time around at the same stop even though I have no request, I find this helps to make the problem go away. Interestingly, someone from the back will come forward to the front door and request the next stop. This is a nice check from the universe this problem has been put to bed because I have not resisted the late ring. I have to be willing to make the stop. And when I am, all is well and the Zen of driving a bus returns.

The Black Hole

THE SEAT OPPOSITE "SHOTGUN," BEHIND the operator's seat, is unofficially called, "the black hole." Folks who sit here become invisible. They cannot see to the front of the bus because their view is blocked. And there is no pull string to activate the chime or stop request. Acoustics are very poor because of the wall behind our driver's seat, and if the blowers are on, it is next to impossible to hear them speak.

There is a large distance in most coaches past the first two hand holds or poles that connect from the ceiling to the seat. If the first four seats on either side are full, especially with passengers with bags, or a walker, a baby, or odd carry-on, it is time to make sure the interior mirror is set to view the no man's land.

Add to this the various nationalities and accents from the melting pot which is San Francisco, and you have a perfect recipe for failure in passing up their request. So, when I have a working mirror which I can point to the black hole, all the better. I can also turn off the blower, or wait until I am stopped to ask them again where they are going, or what stop they need. I have found out the hard way that it is what I can do to fill their need, rather than go into twenty questions about what I do. This was the solution to fill the black hole.

We've also added a roll bar of sorts to the flip up seats mid coach, so we now have a handhold for those sitting in the flip-up seats by the rear door. This is a godsend for those with groceries and carrying bags. Our new coaches even have a leg rest for someone in a leg brace or on crutches!

And so goes the Muniverse! And staying in the Zen!

Boarding the Coach

THE ABILITY TO GET ON a trolley depends on where you look. If you understand the approaching coach is not just a bus, but a person driving a bus, your odds increase dramatically the door will open. Eye contact is key. Most people who have the door closed on them while they are standing by the bus because they are in the blind zone to the left of the front doors and not to the right of the doors where the operator can see.

When the doors are open, the exterior mirrors are almost completely blocked by the doors. Our vision as operators is limited to a narrow sliver about four feet away from the bus in our exterior mirrors, and if allowed by the interior mirror over the doors, about one foot away from the steps. I say allowed because the mirror or mirrors over our front doors do not always stay in place, or turned to a way in which we can see correctly.

Adding cameras over the cockpit and in the front window have been helpful is showing our blind spots to those watching, but their point of view is not the same as from the operator's seat. Most problems in boarding the coach are because the operator's point of view is not considered or understood. We don't want drama any more than you the passenger does.

Sometimes a "helpful" passenger within the coach, or someone outside of the coach tries to aid our view by stating someone is coming to the door, but their point of view is limited by their position as they don't have access to the thirteen mirrors we have on the long trolleys, and the eight mirrors we have on the 40 foot coaches. The number one reason we don't wait for the runner, or acknowledge the late comer is because those being "helpful" don't see traffic conditions or the knowing of the lights as to when a stale green or red overrides holding the door because of safety. Operators have come to know when waiting adds to traffic blocking and delay, especially at intersections like Pine and Van Ness, Greenwich and Van Ness, and other areas like Market and Van Ness where the window of safely pulling away is much narrower than the random late patron boarding in the front. I have found holding all doors open solves much of this problem, as late boarders can enter the rear and tag in rather than wait the time it takes to get to the front, particularly if the bus shelter or some other obstacle hinders vision and boarding.

Motorists, too, would be well to look at our green courtesy lights over the rear doors to see if they go off and signal boarding is complete. These are one of several cues the bus is ready to move. If the car people would understand the beats and patterns of when the bus leaves the zone, fewer abrupt lane changes would be necessary. Less traffic conflict would arise and the horn would not be needed.

One technique I use to get the attention of motorist is turning the wheel to the left when I am ready to move. The turn signal seems to have little effect. *Use of turn signals creates more jams and dangers than a smooth lane transition without one.* If there is a large enough space cushion between a double parked truck or car mid-block, I do use my signal to give any car behind me time to read my left turn signal and pass and be free of being blocked by my large vehicle signature, referred to as billboarding.

In any event, knowing how to board, and being aware of what conditions are ripe for a door close, helps more than you may know. Texting by passengers, or being lost in the music of earphones, does create moral hazard with other passengers who may be more aware of what's happening. It also adds to the danger of collision with other cars when a texter on board asks for a back door after I have already kept the doors open and then waited for the narrow safe time of pull away, only to have to stop and reopen. Many times this is not safe, and those who are late to depart become angry when they are sent to the next stop. There is no legal basis for "kidnapping" on a bus line because our route is findable and predictable. But there are those who like to keep the argument you cannot win in extended drama, with the comment bomb at the end as they leave through the front door, usually without any concept of their part in creating the problem.

If in the Zen, these comments fall flat, and other passengers comment on the fault of the other person and not on the operator. When the thank you's keep coming when people step down, I know I am in the Zen zone.

Sleepers

THE BEST OFFENSE IS A good defense. The best way to prevent someone from being asleep such as a log or dead wood, is to spot the candidates when they board. And even then, there will always be those who come in the back door, or appear alert when they enter. But at 45 minutes a trip, there is plenty of time to fall asleep. Many wonder why the heat is not on when it's cold outside. The answer is: we don't want people falling asleep. The heat makes us drowsy, especially if we are already tired to begin with.

If I anticipate someone falling asleep, I ask them where they are going. If they are going into a deep trance, they won't even look at me or answer the question. I either pop the brake then and there to get them off, which usually doesn't work, or as a gentle reminder I am being of service, let them get the rest they need. Half of the time, they sleep for one terminal only, and get off when I am back in the other direction. And 98 percent of the time, two trips as an unwritten rule, they get off. It is the 2 percent where I have to call central for an inspector or the police.

All I can do is tell my truth the best I know how, and see where the cards fall. But better these cards fall, then the drunk who started drinking at happy hour, and now it is last call! Note to bouncers: have a friend ride with the drunk, so at least we know where to open the door to let our "friend" off! Don't push your problem on to my bus. If you bring a sober friend who knows where the man of the sauce is going, fine. At least I have a destination. We are not a shelter. We are a transportation company. If I know where you are going and you have a destination, I am okay with that. If you can't answer a simple question about where you want to go, then we have a problem. I have learned that popping the brake and getting the destination first, when a drunk or potential sleeper boards, is the best time and place to get an answer. Otherwise it is time to call the cops: hopefully not when I am trying to pull-in and go home.!

Once I called the fire department. Twenty-sixth and Mission is the collection depot on Sunday morning for the ne'er do wells coming down from their latest binge. And nowhere else is the metaphor, "dropping like a rock" more apt. This man was the only one waiting at the stop and I took in a deep breath and sighed in an, "Here we go." He was seething with anger just under the eyes, but was really tired. I guess I just felt sorry for him and thought his being tired was of the greater than his anger, so I let it go. And I know from experience that this is the key to avoiding trouble. But when I tried to rouse him at the end of the line, he wouldn't budge. I asked him to get up and he cursed at me and called me names. He then smugly went back to sleep.

I could choose to ignore him and let him sleep, or get him off. There had been theft of personal items at this terminal, and I needed to use the bathroom. I would have to exit the coach. Because he had fluid dropping from his lower lip, I decided to play the medical emergency card. I called the fire department. He tried the same bull on the firefighters when they tried to get him up, but he was outnumbered and outgunned. Three big guys in full battle array got him up and out, and all I did was dial. Whew. But at what cost to the city?

This is where homelessness and drug use really taxes our city. The cost of these services really adds to the taxpayer bill. But would an assault upon me from an angry passenger also have a cost? Staying in my chair, and calling Central Control for help was and always is, the solution for keeping my job and staying in *The Art of Driving a Bus.*

The Boat People

IN PULLING UP TO CLAY and Drumm on the 1 California, or passing by the Ferry Plaza on the number 6, 14, 21, or 31, I get to pick up the boat people. These are passengers who have come from across the bay on the water to connect to another bus system, or visit a destination within our city. They can be found near the Embarcadero, and almost always have their ferry stub ready to present. I jokingly call these folks the boat people.

And the boat people are great people. They are not bringing another vehicle into the city. If everyone followed this example, the quality of life in San Francisco would improve dramatically.

When the Bay Bridge is closed for repairs or re-striping, usually on Labor Day or a Holiday weekend, traffic in the city is fantastic. Because there is no traffic. I can easily find my door to the curb at every corner, and keep to the schedule. One All Hallows Eve, the bridge was closed all weekend, and getting around was as easy as pie. I always salute those outside of the city who don't bring their vehicle into the city. I make sure they get an adequate transfer time to board another coach, and I answer any questions about the bus routes. Being of service is fun when another person from outside the city can find our bus system as a pleasant alternative to the back-up at the toll plaza.

"Do you go all the way?"

"A coffee date works for me first."

The White Lie

BECAUSE SAN FRANCISCO IS SUCH a small, compact city with water on three sides, our crosstown bus routes intersect with every line that goes downtown inbound, or out to a beach on the ocean or by the bay in the opposite direction. Since we also have a large visitor population, we get asked about directions at the front door when we pull up to a stop. In order to maintain a relaxed Zen-like posture and relaxed state of mind, I have finally learned what the visitors are really asking, based upon what stop they are standing at, and that the white lie saves time and confusion even though what I am saying to them is not literally true.

On the crosstown 33 Stanyan, I head inbound on Haight Street for four blocks before I turn-off on Ashbury to go over the Twin Peaks, Clarendon hill, on my way to the Castro, the Mission, and Potrero, which are all non-downtown neighborhoods. But my direction is outbound, even though I am heading inbound on Haight. The question asked continuously by at least one party of visitors, on Stanyan and Clayton at Haight is, "Do you go to Market Street?" The honest answer is yes. The helpful, not literally true answer is no. After coming down the Clarendon hill, the 33 turns on to Market at it's uppermost point when it becomes renamed as Portola, at what I like to call Dead Man's Curve. We turn almost 180 degrees on a hairpin turn with a vista of downtown and the East Bay. It is a dramatic turn with a very scenic twist. But there are no major destinations or points of interest at this hairpin turn, save for the lovely view.

We then travel down upper Market for about two blocks, and then head for Castro village, which does place us one block from the Market and Castro underground line (Castro Station). Boarding underground connects easily to all downtown areas and eventually to BART. So if they don't appear rushed, and are in sightseeing mode, I say yes, to take them to the hairpin vista. If it is p.m. rush and they have shopping bags, I say no. "Do you go to Market?" really means, "Do you go downtown?" They aren't specifying where on Market they want to go. After asking time and time again where on Market they want to go, I have come to the conclusion they mean somewhere along 4th or 5th and Market, and Powell Station.

So I have learned to say no, and ask them to wait for the 7R. Or walk down to Masonic for the 6, especially if a 7R has just passed. If I am without a leader, and I am running heavy and late, I always say no. This is how we can control our load when carrying passengers who would normally have boarded the coach in front of me.

Same is true on Potrero Blvd., which is like the old business loop highway that was the main road before the freeway was built. People ask along the thoroughfare if I go to Market. Once again, after much experience, I have found the simplest way to move along is to say no. Wait for the number 9. Which really means I don't go downtown to the Union Square area. The 33 does go to Market and 18th Street, but this is not downtown: it is a residential area miles from downtown. So yes, I do go to Market, but not downtown.

So I find myself having learned what people need by their questions, to answer no, and save time by not going through other questions that add to a delay. Experience with the time of day, how they are dressed, and the regularity of the same question over and over, keeps me talking less, and in a mode to help those who have a destination along my crosstown route. I default to the nearest stop when they ask the open question of a specific business, such as the golden arches. I pass-by two golden arches, three Safeway grocery stores, and three hospitals. I can answer yes, and call out the first one I pass-by.

Usually, most people recognize where they are when they get to the stop they need. Describing the landmarks is usually unnecessary. I don't need to use sarcastic humor, because it can backfire and lead to a bad experience. I learned early on there will never be an end to the same questions being asked over and over, so conserving my response is the easiest way to staying in the Zen zone.

What It's Really About

WHENEVER THERE IS A PROBLEM on the bus, I have to ask myself, how important is this really? Would I rather be calm or would I rather be right? And giving the space to wait until someone comes forward to complain keeps incidents few and far between. Only when someone has a complaint am I to act. And how I handle the situation either makes it go away or get worse.

The first thing to do when a fight looks ready, is to open the rear doors and pop the brake. The sound of the brake let's everyone know we aren't moving. The rear door open gives an out to one of the people in the argument. Since impatience is usually the prevailing mood, one of the party leaves. If they don't, I can ask one of the folks to come up to sit by me. Or state there is another coach in a few minutes, and you might find this to be a more comfortable ride.

All in all, I have to check my mental state and ask myself am I being of service to those in the coach, or do I have an agenda based on some sort of fear about what I think may or may not happen. But a word of advice: Don't feed the pigeons. That is, don't feed into a senseless argument. Do not respond to the Borg. *Resistance is futile.*

As time has given me insight, I do have an intuition about how far people are traveling on the coach. I can spot the problem child before they board. And I can guess where they will most likely get off. Their destination on the Mission is: 16th Street. A rush to the door usually results when they see their dealer on a nearby street. "Is this an emergency?" I ask. When they shout, "Yes!" I can use the rules to my advantage, and get rid of them, being careful there is no threat of an oncoming skater or cyclist. This impatience energy is one full of mishap and accident. By asking them to come to the front door, I interrupt that energy and make it safer. But only if getting them off the coach will improve the mood of the coach of everyone else riding. It is when the request for a back door is out of synch with the lights and the traffic, that I move the coach forward, a little bit, to bring the doors to a safe place while signaling to traffic behind me I am not moving away.

Usually people get loudest before they depart. If they are arguing when they get on, I have to let it settle right then and there, or avoid them getting on in the first place. I have learned when the music or the voices get the loudest it is either a cry for help, or a deep need to be heard. Or a revolutionary protest and rage against the machine, in this case, the Municipal Railway, for which gratitude has been lost. We now return you to *The Art of Driving a Bus*, already in progress!

Move Up Four

WHEN A COACH GOES OUT of service in front of me, it means my headway has doubled. So in order to minimize the impact of no leader, we are allowed to split the headway and move up. Most move ups are made over the radio, and are usually two, three, or four minutes. Sometimes we know we have lost our leader before Central Control knows. Other times, we are in the dark, and rely on the radio contact from the operator who goes out of service, to call Central Control, and hope we are given timely information to move up before we find out the hard way. And it wasn't till I talked to an inspector about headway, that the "science" of move ups was a standard operating order based on the headways between buses on the various lines during the various four hour headway windows. It had never occurred to me headway move ups were standardized, and I could learn a lot by knowing what supervisors were trained to know when they were trained.

In fact, much of what I am writing here is based upon my experience and observations which may contain gaps in knowledge known by my superiors. And much of my knowledge was less complete than I first admitted. Those in charge were actually a lot more knowledgeable about what was going on than I was from my limited point of view behind the wheel. Most conflict arises out of misplaced desire. And my desire to run on time was actually misplaced because I was not aware, for example, that I did not have a bus running behind me, and that I should not move up because I would be creating a hole behind me.

On rare occasion, I am informed I have triple headway, and oddly enough, I found myself less anxious and more grateful than if I was just missing one bus in front of me.

Because of what I call the seven minute rule: That in seven minutes, many waiting for the bus start to make other choices; get on another bus, take a cab, or walk to another bus line. When push comes to shove, there is a magic moment, when the ability to make the schedule is so impossible, there is no longer the need to try to make it work. And as the coach fills up early, it becomes obvious there is no way to try to pick everyone up. In fact, the hard part of a move up of four, is when it may or may not be possible to pick everyone up: the point at which to pass up may not be so clear. For example, can I pick up those five people, or will this create havoc at the next stop? Should I keep it crowded for the next two blocks, or should I start reducing my load now?

There are very clear rules about when to stop passing up. When the bus is full, one must pass up stops. But sometimes the number of people in the aisle can be variable. Is the crowd mostly young, or are their people with canes and walkers on board? The demographics of who is on board is also a factor to consider a pass–up. Sure, I may have some room for a few youngsters in the back, but if a large group of seniors with grocery carts is waiting at the next stop, and there is no room in the aisle in the front, the stop is not going to go well. Where I stop the coach and place the doors, comes into play in conditions like this. When in doubt, make the stop, following my general orders, but do so in a way that adjusts the load. If I pull forward in the zone intending passengers can see if there is a coach behind me (usually emptier). Also those with a valid card can enter and tag-in on the rear doors. This skill really helps avoid the, "please move back," which very rarely works. Actions speak louder than words is a principle that works well here. It isn't what I say, but what I do that makes the art of driving much easier.

Back Door!

THE GREEN LIGHT HAS BEEN on over the back door for at least 20 seconds. A large number of passengers have departed thru the back door, and entered in the front. The kneeler was used for the nice grandma, and bikes were loaded on the front rack. Or someone takes a bike off of the front rack that does not belong to them! It is at these times that the cry comes from within the masses at the back of the bus, "Back Door!"

And if I am in the Zen of the moment, I have anticipated this delay, and can turn on the green light and look in my rear mirror to see the rear doors opening from someone stepping down. But sometimes the battle cry comes too late, or I can't hear the call from the back because of the crush of humanity absorbing any sound from that far away. Or the blowers are on and the acoustics are poor, and I have already started moving on to the next stop. But I have also found that to continue on to the next stop without letting the doors reopen, also results in bad blood that does not have to be. If I can turn on the green light for the back door, and relieve the tension, all the better. There is nothing worse than an angry passenger pushing to the front to confront me on why I turned off the back door switch, and prevented disembarking.

So the key, when crowded is to pause, turn off the light, and see if I hear a "back door!" The contradiction is that just when I desire to pull away to keep my headway from getting longer is exactly when this back door problem arises. With the number of people on board increasing, so too does the delay occur with folks heading to the back door. So I have just one last word: when packed, stacked and racked, try moving to the back door a block in advance. Granted, you don't have to stand right by the door, but at least get ready to find the flow that starts when people start stepping down. On the older, longer trolleys, the toggle to open all doors is a life saver to keeping time in the zone shorter, and I also find fewer problems with the doors when I keep the rear doors standing open for those one or two second beats that prevents the doors from being forced or damaged.

"The middle step is the abracadabra mechanism when the green light is on." or "Step down for open sesame when the green light is on." If the PA is not working or is turned up too loud or not with any sound at all, I can always hit the toggle to open the doors anyway. Tourists or those first timers don't understand how to activate the rear door mechanism, and sometimes they find themselves on to the next stop if I can't see them when the coach is crowded. But the simple cry of "back door!" is the quickest way to see the green light come on, or have the doors opened manually. Pushing on the doors or staring at them does not usually make them open.

When youngsters are loaded from after school, and I have a good PA, I remind them to stay clear of the rear doors. True, the doors are strong in and of themselves, but the hinge mechanism, and the brushes and air delivery system which powers them, is very fragile and weak. By toggling the rear door to stand open at every stop, so that the door opens automatically, even if no one is getting off, does signal to the youth who is leaning on the door with a backpack, that it is not a good idea, and they stop leaning. Once again, what I do rather than what I say, seems to work best.

Screaming or yelling at the operator may not work as an abracadabra mechanism. Seeing green and not putting off or putting out red is a sure sign the driver is in the Zen zone behind the wheel!

Dump and Run

At first, it would seem this is a rude action, and that this chapter may contain inappropriate material not suited for young audiences. But happily this is not the case. In fact, dump and run, when practiced flawlessly, is a thing of beauty that has me in the grateful, creative mode which places me firmly in the Zen zone.

When an intending passenger runs diagonally across several lanes of moving traffic, smiles and waves at me and madly dashes to the front door, just as the traffic breaks, or the light turns green, they have the distinct honor of being the passenger of the day. A quick flash of the fast pass, already in hand, or a perfect swipe of the tag in card, and they definitely have passenger of the day in the bag. Someone with quarters counted, already in hand, with the perfect waterfall method of slipping them down the slot, wins first place.

And this was a trip to get over. I was getting angry and in a scold mode to tell them that their actions were not safe. And it kept happening over and over. What I resist persists. I learned to calmly state, "Hey, that wasn't safe. I couldn't see you when you came from behind in my blind spot. You may not be picked-up because unsafe behavior is not rewarded with a ride." So as soon as I got over myself as being Mister Safety, all these late rushes stopped coming. As with the bum rush to the front door before arriving at the curb. I can always delay opening the front door and let those who migrate in the aisle see that they can depart faster if they go out the back door. Once again, what I do, and not what I say has a beneficial effect. Controlling the load inside my coach by delaying the opening of the front door has helped.

So here in the city, we have a unwritten rule of conduct about crossing the street to catch a Muni bus. If the sign says don't walk, and the red hand starts flashing, do what the sign says, run like hell! Also if the white icon is solid. Pay it no never mind. In fact, you can look anywhere but in the oncoming lane of traffic, and be content in realizing that the cars must yield to you. Hah! The haughtiness and entitlement pedestrians have when crossing the street is second to none in San Francisco. But I don't advise this sentiment when crossing near an off ramp from the freeway, especially on weekends. One young man was killed for this misjudgment. Out of town drivers, unfamiliar with our provencal attitudes, may have not yet been "trained" on how to drive in our city.

Indeed, looking at the license plates, especially with the name of the dealer or city on the trim ring around the plate, speaks volumes about where the car and it's driver are coming from. If you see an SUV with a Dublin or Pleasanton tag, give wide berth! San Francisco is rare in that pedestrian sentiment has not changed from the earlier days when trolleys were king, and the car was a novelty for Sunday rides..

Perfect timing, with no delay. Now that is definitely the Zen of Driving A Bus.

Seniors Come Out

AND THEN THE RAINS CAME. And no one had an umbrella. And no one was dressed for the cold downpour. And socks got wet. And shoes got ruined. And it rained for forty days and forty nights. Actually, was it in 2006 when we had 44 days of rain? From the Fourth of July to some time before the Blue Angels in October the sun never came out. Not even like in Seattle where at least you get an hour or two of sunlight in the afternoon. And then the weather breaks, and its beautiful. And here comes everyone and his brother to do errands, get the pantry caught up, or go to the doctor's office, or the post office, or a million and one other things where taking the bus is a must. Not for those who can bike, walk, or run, but those with mobility problems or strollers, or shopping carts from hell. And the kneeler is needed at every stop, and you had better wait till I sit down, and blah blah blah. Everyone comes out at once, and you may as well throw the schedule out the window.

Truth be told, the weather effect only holds for about three days. Or for a few weeks after the change to the rainy season. Because once people re find their umbrella, or galoshes, or their rain jacket after the first storm of the year, then everyone adapts quickly, and the weather no longer becomes a threat, or an excuse to not take the bus.

But if there are two nasty days of weather, which in San Francisco means biting cold fog, or heavy monsoon like rain, you can bet the pent up demand to go out and get things done, builds, so that by day three, if the weather turns, as it usually does, out come the ancient ones and the rule of law, the rule of God. Respect your elders, and give them the time they need to board and find a seat. And if a lift request is needed, be sure to wait until they have found a place for their cart, or are clicked in by the flip down seat. And I have been in trouble for making the light before they are seated or locked. And I am very gentle in starting the roll, yet I don't understand why they can't feel the difference I bring. I am very gently starting, and don't push past walking the dog until they are sitting down. The most problems I have with angry passengers are those who don't seem to be able to tell my starts are smooth and slow. Of course, there are those times too, when the points of power are set higher than most, and I am turning the wheel to the left, and I hear the apples and bananas ripping thru paper bags and thuds and duds falling and rolling around in the aisle. Or the sound of a cane dropping to the floor as gasps go up throughout the coach. And I dread to turn and ask, "Is everyone okay back there?"

Most falls on board do seem to be random and unexpected. If a senior disappears from sight (and that's not hard to do when the aisle is crowded) because they are usually shorter or smaller, they enter in to the purgatory area before the rear door where there are no hand holds. This is called no-man's land. If they are carrying something in their hand, such as a bag or a cart, it makes for an unstable and unsafe situation. Being in the Zen zone means I am using my interior center mirror to make sure everyone is settled before I move the coach.

Reroute In-Effect

IN THE STAR TREK MOVIE, *The Search for Spock,* the famous line, "The needs of the many outweigh the needs of the one," is no more self evident in the transit schedule, especially during special events. Some regular bus stops have a rider alert bulletin posted on the bus shelter, or on a utility pole. One of the failures about re-routing buses seems to be that the needs of the many are dismissed for the needs of the few, or the one. It makes no sense to send a bus around an area that is congested from a special event, thereby throwing off the schedule and creating irregular headway between buses.

When the Castro neighborhood streets are blocked off for Halloween, or New Year's Eve, the 33 is sent over one block to 19th Street, which is up a steep hill with lots of parked cars. Traffic becomes gridlocked and is forced onto nearby streets. Turns on the bus are stressful because we have to cross the centerline and violate our space cushion.

A recent fatality involved a motor coach being taken off its route prematurely and forced on to a small alleyway in high pedestrian traffic. Whenever a bus travels along a route that is unanticipated by regular pedestrian and traffic flow, the chance for an accident goes way up. The cost of litigation and claims paid far exceed the "cost" of placing the motor coach far enough away to avoid the congestion and narrow side street bypass.

Choices made by Street Operations as directed by Central Control very rarely look at the safety choices and the affect upon the operators' mind and stress level. Most reroutes, if taken a few blocks farther, travel on clear traffic streets and without delay.

Any delay of two or three coaches puts a "black hole" in headway that creates more work for inspectors, and sometime takes up to two hours to fully correct at the following terminals for that line. And there seems to be no clear communication procedure to learn from the mistakes of the past.

Fires and the blocked streets from the service vehicles, also create havoc, with instructions for re-route are either impossible or not safe. Our buses can travel short distances without being on the wires. But more often than not, the topography of the area is not taken into account. If our buses are full of passengers, our battery power does not go far, and the bus can't make the upgrade because the auxiliary power unit is not strong enough to move the coach when it is heavy. Coaches become sequestered along the blocked off street, and the Schedule fails.

If operator's faith that re-routes were done from the point of view of keeping buses running and free of congestion, we might be able to make a big difference. Muni is really good in getting diesel shuttles to an area where trolleys are blocked, but I would hope that standard re-routes were in place and understood by all, so that operator's would be given the standing orders to make a decision to steer clear of the congestion point and report conditions immediately. Bus drivers aren't able to suggest re-routes. It must be done by a supervisor on the scene. But the minutes of delay become magnified into hours, if the re-route comes after trolleys are already blocked. And it is during these times that the eyes on the road from an operator become helpful by calling Central Control. This is when having a professional attitude when using the radio can be a make or break perception of good relations with those who have a challenging job to keep trolleys rolling without being able to see what is happening. Staying out of trouble and getting the needed switchback from Central becomes a future credit when the time comes for needed support, even if they can't see you.

Special Events

FINDING THE ZEN ZONE DURING special events can be a challenge. Such as doing the 21 Line by Golden Gate Park on the weekend of a major concert or running event that ends or lets out near the Polo Fields in the park.

I had made a wise choice to work the 21 line on weekends in the summer because I vowed never again to do the number 5 on summer weekends, ever. And so while I was waiting to leave my terminal by the park, I saw a number 5 packed with people pull up beside me. The operator was hollering she was not going to Market, and to get on my bus. Truth was, she was going to Market, just not to Powell Station. All the concertgoers could just as easily walked to Civic Center station or to Powell from her short terminal at Jones and Mc Allister, but she wasn't having it. No one was listening and no one was getting off her bus. She was experiencing that part of Packed Stacked and Racked where no one moves or listens because, they were lucky enough to get on a bus and be damned if they got off their lucky ticket to ride.

Feeling her pain, and not upset about taking on her passengers, I got out of my bus to coax some of those on her bus to get on mine which was traveling in the same direction to Market Street. But no one was biting. I had a completely empty bus but no one would get off. Here is where past experience about being passed up by full buses, puts lead in the feet of all passengers, and no amount of verbal instruction helps. These folks were able to "cheat death" and fit on to her bus, beating out who knows how many unlucky souls. And they would be damned if they were going to be suckered off of a coach they had so victoriously boarded. No, in this case, no one was falling for it. They knew they were going downtown, and that was the end of it!

I tried to get the operator to change her statement about going to Market, or to relax about her announcement, but the only thing that would have had let people off her coach would be to go out of service. In hindsight, this is what I should have proposed to her by her drivers' side window. "Oh, look your air is low and you can't legally proceed. Ask everyone to board my coach." That would have given her breathing room to start picking up with an empty bus, and I could have continued with my shorter distance, full, but not in an agitated state of mind. I have always sought to give a break to an operator who is overwhelmed because I know there are times when I am in that predicament, and nothing good comes from it. Learning how to give and gain the respect of my coworkers is perhaps the most and last challenging aspect of staying in the Zen of driving transit in San Francisco.

New Year's Eve

HALLOWEEN IS ONLY THREE DAYS away as I write this chapter, and it's a Saturday and already I have seen costumes last night, and even earlier in the week. But the holiday season vibe is picking up and everyone is in the change of gears of the season. The air is crisp and clear. The trees and grasses are making themselves known in the warm still afternoon air by the scent they let out as we walk by. But I don't know about you, but when I recall working on All Hallows Eve, and driving through the Castro on the 24 or the 33, my brain jumps ahead to the next disaster, New Year's Eve. For some reason, especially on New Year's Eve, there is the prevalent thought to let it all go. But now, not having had a drink in 17 years, and not really missing it at all, I begin to see a false promise about New Year's Eve. What the heck is the deal for a calendar click, and why does it call for a drink?

But of course, to celebrate the New Year. Oh, yeah. But you might find that transit operators have a different idea about it if working on New Year's Eve! Perhaps this title should read, "You Get What You Pay For." If Muni is free from 8 p.m. on, what do we know from experience about things that are free? Such as the futon frames we see scattered on our sidewalks, or the Christmas trees on the corner on January 7th? Worthless. Those riding home at 9 p.m., great deal. But as 10:30 p.m. approaches, and folks are headed out to party, the buses become not unlike the 8x in Chinatown, packed. And so on to the most memorable story I have about New Year's Eve, or should I say, New Year's morning, at about 2 a.m.

121

There on the island on Duboce, just outside of the tunnel, stood over 100 people taking every square inch of the island. And this is a two-car island. With overflow intending passengers waiting on the curbside sidewalk. But trains leaving downtown and the Ferry Plaza fireworks were exiting the tunnel and going out of service to return to the barn at Balboa Park. The cars were full and dumping off more people to wait to go out to the avenues and the Sunset. Muni's free service ended at midnight that year, I think it was 2009, and only the regular motor coach N Judah service remained. One standard diesel bus every half hour. It doesn't take a genius to figure out that one standard forty foot motor coach every half hour, does not cover those coming from two car light rail vehicles every ten minutes.

I was pulling-in on the 22 line and gasped at the huge crowd waiting at Duboce and Church. Once again relieved that I was a crosstown line. And to my horror of horrors, I looked left at Market and saw a young lady driving an outbound N Judah motor coach on Market, ready to make the turn to Church and then left to Duboce. Oh my God. If ever there was a ninth level of hell this was it. She had a relatively empty bus, as those downtown were taking the underground to head away. If I could relive this moment, I would have run to her coach at the light before she turned to Church and warned her about what lay ahead on Duboce. Take the Haight Street route and don't look to the left! Put on your neutral face and pray you can make it through the stop sign! I never knew what happened, but suffice it to say it was not pretty. This operator, who ever she is, should win some kind of hero's medal of honor for having to make her next stop. I read in the paper the next Monday about complaints about owl service, but nothing, nothing, in writing the day after, could do justice for the battle cry that must have gone up when she made the turn to the island. All I can say is girl, you deserve a vacation to Hawaii or some other fantastic place. Whew! It was really cold that night, and I wonder how her next trip went. Peace be with you!

The Bigger They Are . . .

"THE BIGGER THEY ARE THE harder they fall" seems to be completely unrelated to this, but after filling out the number of accident reports I have over the years, I think somehow this does seem to matter. Every occurrence relates to what I was first told in my final interview upon hiring, and in my classroom training during the discussion on accidents and writing the accident report. It is the only class that has stood out in my mind over the years; and was a very clear take on what this job meant as a part of our larger economy, and was so right to the core that even through challenging contract negotiations over the years with our union and management, and even with public comment in the news, these words still, to me, ring true.

This was during the mid to late nineties when Netscape was the Godsend, and Yahoo was unstoppable. "Yes, they have great stock options and a creative workspace, but what they don't have is your longevity at one job." And other senior operators in various classes at the training department, and even in the Gilley room, have echoed this sentiment in a slightly different way with the simple encouragement to, "Stick around and see how it goes." My favorite is, "Sit Back and Watch the Show!"

I identified with this on a deep level, and I am glad I did. No matter how hard this job was to be, no matter how awful I thought it was, was to persevere and keep at it. And sure enough, just like any other job, I started to see the repeats. The patterns of the same thing happening over and over, and how to deal with whatever, became a natural working part of my mind.

This one trait I have learned from my Grandfather who was up early every day to commute into New York City to work for Con Edison, from my Dad behind his desk in the study to prepare another grant request to the National Institute of Health, and from Wilton who got up at 5 a.m. to work in the shipyards at Newport News: keep on trudging. All these men had something in common: they never received any accolades or promotion for their steady paced work, but they kept at the same job for all of their life.

And that steady paycheck was something I never really had, with like 8 W-2s during I think it was 1978, or the five I had in 1987! My heart goes out to any young person struggling in their teens or twenties who doesn't see the benefit and simplicity of keeping to the grindstone for a period of time like years instead of months. The fallacy of cut and run, whereby I quickly grasp a job description, and then move on, was not the real truth. Overcoming challenges and seeing them through were actually more important for long range skills in developing intimacy with others.

To be sure, I also envy the youth aspect of trying different things, but at some point, I realized my life could be simpler if I just kept to one thing at a time, and gave it more time than I thought I should. Walking off a job in 40 minutes or after one day, seemed to be more of my modus operandi, than to wade through difficulty and ask for help. If I could have just waited it out to get a few suggestions on how to break down a task into smaller parts to see past the other side of failure. If any sidebar to this chapter exists, it would have to be to put young brashness aside to get feedback about what has worked in the past for others. And the cost of this simple action, to ask for help, which is to say, to not ask for help, has probably been the largest missed opportunity cost in my life which could have saved me lots of grief.

To get back to the training class, I vividly remember our instructor's first question to our group of cadets, if you will, freshly being minted by the city to become a transit operator. The instructor asked, "What is the first thing I have read time and time again on accident reports, or heard from an operator in a conversation about and accident?" And what confuses me and has left me completely confounded year after year, even though I piped up with the correct answer as soon as he asked it, was the lack of simplicity and clarity I possessed in writing out my reports. I always wondered why it took so long for the division trainer to grade my report. Now, I get my answer about an accident within a day or two from the accident. And I could not see why other operators knew why this was happening, and why they got their verdicts so much quicker than I did. And I have been teased and mocked to almost no end about the *War and Peace*, or *Gone With The Wind*, lengthy essays on my reports. I talk too long and I write too much, and my only surmise is because I am too much a thinker, and spend too much time in my head. I guess it's why I am enjoying this book so much. I get to get it out of my head; all the stuff kept in there, without ever putting the pen to paper, and thus clearing my own internal hard drive.

Most of my prose in the accident report was always assuming what the other driver, pedestrian, or cyclist was thinking, or why they did what they did. In true Joe Friday Dragnet form, did I need to hear, "Just the facts, just the facts." Because this is where my disconnect comes from. To keep it simple, and just report what happened, not what I think happened. I loved the Dispatcher's reaction to my reports: rolling their eyes and handing it back to me, or their frustration at having no room to sign the report because my words bled over into their section. This was helpful in seeing I needed to cut down the verbiage, and at one point, I realized I should do a rough draft of just the accident description part of the form, and then, after feedback from the dispatcher, rewrite it shorter and simpler, about what actually happened, without all the guesswork about why people did what they did. So, even though I got the answer right away in my first accident class with our instructor, I did appear clueless many years later in reducing the report to the simple actions leading to sideswipe, t-bone, squeeze play, or fixed object. If I could have read

125

other reports, or known the simple food groups of how accidents are classified, I would hopefully have done better, but I am not counting on it!

So have you guessed what the simple answer was and is? Cue Steve Harvey in Family Feud, to say we polled a recent transit operator class and got their best response to, "What does a person say after having a collision or accident?" Answer Is: "I didn't see you!"

"The car just came out of nowhere." And blah, blah, blah. So I make sure I am checking side to side, left-right-left, so there is no guesswork about who is encroaching on my lane, my territory. And tracking rate-of-speed is the best way to guess when a motorist is going to make a foolish unsafe move. Impatience can usually be seen a mile a way when sight lines are clear. But in congested, built-up San Francisco, we usually have limited sight distance. Buildings come right up to the corner, or there is almost always a beer truck, bakery truck, or parcel delivery truck parked on the curb or double parked, right up against a crosswalk or corner. And this is where considering, The Bigger You Are, the Harder They Fall, really becomes important. The transit professional has a word for this when this happens: it is called billboarding. You can't see the forest for the trees, and there is little reaction space to avert a threat that comes from behind the obstacle. Use of the friendly toot, or light flash can be useful, but the bottom line is to adjust by slowing down.

And in the career flow of office politics, it probably doesn't hurt to employ this idea to your job and duties. No one really knew what I was doing in all the cleaning of the bins in back storerooms, but, tooting one's horn about getting things done, may be helpful to make sure the right person knows where the credit is due. This can apply towards future job evaluations, and moving up to the bigger office.

The Argument You Cannot Win

A GOOD BUS DRIVER SHOULD be seen and not heard. Well, I certainly don't fall into this category, no way. Most operators follow the golden rule of: Information gladly given but safety requires avoiding unnecessary conversation. When a passenger wants to "be right," the best advice is to let them "win," so I can once again reduce the distraction and move-on. If I have asked to see their transfer, and they show it in such a way that I cannot see the time or the day, I ask for the regular fare. If they become angry when they hold the transfer in my face, I say thank you, and this usually ends the drama. But there are those who must enjoy confrontation, and being right. "I am sorry, but I did not see your transfer when you first showed it to me." By this time I am wondering why I asked for the fare in the first place, but I always check my inflection and voice to make sure I am being neutral in my tone. But even still, this has no effect, and some question me as to why I am being so rude. And this brings me to the argument you cannot win. I don't see why they are calling me rude. I am just doing my job. And even when another passenger comes to my aid by saying that I am just doing my job, this has little effect on the drama.

If someone has a "helpful" suggestion on how to get to a destination, and they already have my answer, fine. I have learned I don't need to argue the point. Everyone has a different pattern that works for them on how to get from point a to point b. Since Muni has so many different lines, when a question is asked about how to get somewhere, different answers come every time another person is asked. It is not that anyone is lying. It is just there are so many ways to skin a cat to get to where you want to go.

We don't have eyes in the back of our head, and we are not mind readers. If riders cannot show me their fare before they cross the yellow line, all I am required to do is to state the fare. Usually they don't acknowledge me at all. And I have found this is actually a good thing. It is not on me to be the policeman for the fare. We have fare inspectors for that. When I let go of judging them and trust it is not up to me to determine if they are being honest or not, my day goes much better. The less drama the better. I am a bus driver and not a stage performer on Broadway. Though I have been on Broadway for one block between Fillmore and Steiner when I am on a run on the 22 line, I usually am not on stage! Keep me in the Zen, and oh by the way, if you look over and to your left you will see Mrs. Doubtfire's house.

The Stroller Incident

WITHOUT EVEN HAVING READ THIS chapter, I am sure there are operators who once they saw this subheading, rolled their eyes to the back of their head. Likewise, regular riders of the 22 Fillmore certainly have paragraphs of stories they could add to this chapter. Anyone who has rode past Fillmore and Haight has the story of the "stroller incident."

When a mom and her armada awaits to board, I have to take in a deep breath, here goes. Please stand by. Perhaps we could put up a test screen. The kids can stand by the door and block, or be told in no uncertain words to MOVE and GET IN THE BUS. And there they stand, looking up in their innocent eyes, why me? And the stroller is now ready to bulldoze through the aisle, which is great with me because moving to the rear gets the bus out of the zone and moving down the road. But heaven help the poor unsuspecting student with their ear buds' music on full blast in a multitask texting mode, or the senior with sore legs and weak knees having the fully loaded stroller run over their toes. And the wrath of the mother yelling to get (the fuck) out (of) the way and don't tell me what to do, bitch.

But not all stroller incidents involve the mom being angry. The other type of stroller incident involves the all too common conflict of interest on who has a higher priority to use the front seats. When a large stroller and mom are boarding, I make sure she moves past the first chairs to the flip top area where wheel chairs go. Popping the brake, standing up and leaving the cockpit to flip up the wheelchair seats is a mind saver in avoiding future conflict. By being out of my seat and asking the one person to vacate for an incoming oversize object, works faster and better when I am present in the here and now. Usually, the person sitting in the area got on when seats were plentiful and "cheap," and is not a disabled person. I have found out the hard way that leaving the aisle blocked with carts, strollers, fishing rods, surfboards, trikes, or Lord Knows What, adds to the likelihood of Fall On Board, and a reset of my safe driving record. As to those with oversize objects waiting in the zone. . .

. . .all I can say about this is the question, "What were you doing when you saw the bus was to arrive in 2 minutes?" Or "What were you doing while you were waiting for the bus?" Now, in all fairness, mom's have a million and one things to be keeping track of, but perhaps that may be part of the problem. Certain stroller manufacturers make strollers not unlike an armored personnel carriers made for the military. And the gondolas of diapers, bottles, and playthings can turn a simple carriage into a military industrial complex.

And so the best advice I can give is: bring help, or carry a lighter load. Usually those who have never taken transit before and are going to the park for the first time on a bus, are the ones who take a long time. And I find if I take an effort to help, all goes well. Am I a part of the solution, or a part of the problem? Often, someone at the stop is there to help. But it is when the coach is full and everyone has on their coat of arms, that problems such as the stroller incident occur. Do tell.

Moms and Babies

AFTER MORNING RUSH OUT COME the moms and babies. Well, sometimes they are on morning rush if the day care center is on your way inbound. But generally, the babes come out from 10 a.m. to noon, or before school gets out around 3 p.m. What a wonder to see a newborns' face. Or even better, the toddlers who look up with wonder, or climb fast to get first dibs on the best seat. And here is where I believe recruitment begins. Get them to see and observe the bus driver as a friend early on, because you never know what sort of impact it will have down the road.

I usually recall my first experiences on the bus or subway when I was young. I always wanted to sit in the front seat. And sure enough I see boys doing the same thing on my bus. Or on an almost empty bus, the race to the back seat. And the mom's comments about what not to do. I enjoy the occasional moment of perfect timing when I have a captive audience of young eyes and mom is distracted by someone or something else and I have them in my grip. "Now I want you to run as fast as you can to the back seat." And to see their eyes light up as finally they get to do what they wanted to do in the first place. And it's really fun on a bus that is sixty feet long. This is when mom is busy folding or prepping the stroller or the million and one other things she is carrying, that use of the diversion is a plus. Usually a nice young man helps out the mom with all the items she has to juggle just to get to the steps, much less climb.

But my complacency is sometimes rudely awakened. A senior with a bag was boarding a few stops after I had boarded a stroller. I had asked the mom to move back behind the wheel well which is located under the first two seats. The first two seats are higher off the aisle because of the wheels underneath. And when push comes to shove, there is no space for dangling legs or stroller wheels to go. If someone runs into a leg or a cart, there is no space under the seat to act as a cushion for extra movement. I had asked her to move back, and she obliged, but not past "no man's land," and not to the flip up seats. I should have raised the chairs up for her stroller, because when the wheels are locked, everything is kosher for any new seniors with a load, because there are still other seats available.

Well, my attention was drifting, and when the senior tried to sit, he was blocked by the stroller. The senior became angry at my allowing the stroller to be in the blue zone, or area for seniors. Whoops. Many times, awakening the baby by taking them out of the stroller creates a scene. A scene complete with sound effects. Wailing, screaming sound effects. Let 'sleeping dogs' lie has always been a good call for a child who is seen but not heard, but this can backfire later with more seniors boarding as we get closer to downtown. Making sure the space in the front stays clear is the best defense, and keeps the Zen.

Always In Service

UNLIKE MOTOR COACHES, TROLLEYS ARE always in service. This is in the rulebook although very few people understand this. If I put up the sign that says "Garage," it does not mean I will not pick you up. I am putting up "Garage" so you can see my destination clearly. Many times when I put up the short destination, people don't see my short line destination stop. I have been written up for posting "Garage."

The street inspectors don't understand that when I put up "Garage," it does not mean I am out of service. The street ops person does not realize I am trying to make my job easier by not confusing passengers, and I am trying to telegraph I am not a regular line coach. We do have the sign, "Ask Driver," but on the old coaches, the line sign still stays up.

I guess most operators, when they put up "Garage," don't stop to pick up people who are waiting. I know I sometimes put up "Garage" when I have had a long day, and am tired. If I have been missing a leader for more than a trip, and have carried a heavy load and been late on schedule, I have been known to put up "Garage" because I believe I have done more than my fair share for the day. I don't feel like dealing with more questions about where I am going after a killer day. The last thing I want to have happen is get in an argument with someone who wants to go farther than my pull in point.

There are times when I announce my last stop and someone comes forward to ask if it is okay if they go with me say to 17th and Bryant. I have always, and without hesitation, said "yes." Because I am a trolley man. And trolleys are always in service. When I have an Eleventh Street destination outbound from Ferry Plaza on the 14 Mission, and I pull into the zone at 9th Street, I announce that this is my last curb on Mission. Notice I say last curb. This is accurate and simple. I did not say this is my last outbound street stop. We click left at 10th and turn on Howard before we turn left on to 11th, but we don't have a sign that says Ninth. It seems short of the mark. In just two blocks, there is the option to get on 4 buses during the day, or two buses at night. But no matter how sincere or patient I am, this message is lost due to language barriers or inattention.

I heard another operator getting into some trouble to pass-up a wheelchair or lift request such as at Fourth Street or at Sixth, because "I am only going to Ninth," just as I had done on an earlier sign-up. This was the same man in a wheelchair, who time after time got passed up or brushed off because we operators assumed he was going to ride beyond our pull-in. He was fast boarding and departing and really did not take up much extra time. Over the years, he became adroit at getting the coach and run number of operators who did not pick him up.

This has led to many complaints for many different drivers, when our rush to be done caused us to get a complaint, a letter, or mail from the dispatcher, a 'love letter,' so to speak, because this was a valid complaint because we passed up a customer with a right to get to our short line destination. After the angry cries from those I shut the door on my quick passes outbound to Ninth, I vowed to put up 'Garage' on my head sign. I realized eventually, it was emotionally much easier to take my time and let everyone board, but let them know I was a short line coach. And how to talk quickly and without lying.

Sure enough, the one wheel chair passenger waiting at Sixth or sometimes Seventh, did want to go to Ninth, and I would never have allowed this ride to occur if I barrelled on ahead without time for those waiting to tell me the short ride was okay and that they were only going to Ninth.

I have found I almost always have one or two passengers who are willing to travel beyond my last regular stop, and in 18 years, I have never had a problem in doing this. A wonderful victory was a nice man in a wheelchair from Larkspur who rode the ferry into my terminal at the Ferry Plaza and after small conversation, found out he wanted to go to Costco at 11th and Harrison. This was on my pull-in route. What a great feeling to take him beyond Mission Street and drop him across the street from Costco, without him having to make a transfer and waste time looking for the 9 line or 47. Being able to get to this point of finding a joy that remains hidden when most of us pull in with a one track mind, has a lot to do with the spirit behind writing this 'how to' manual on the Zen of San Francisco transit.

Our car culture lacks the sense of community built on the bus when we talk and communicate with one another. I still have this man's business card he gave me when he got off at Harrison and 11th. I found out about the history of his nice apartment complex, and his life after retiring to a great place to live. And all this richness would have been lost, or reduced to a piece of mail warranting a conference with my superintendent for possible discipline, when instead, I got a connection from another passenger who got great service.

When pulling-in on the Mission wires from the other direction, the same dilemma occurs at 26th and Mission. We click right, on to 25th, to use the pull-in wires on S. Van Ness. I travel all the way down to 17th Street and S. Van Ness, which is only one block away from 17th and Mission. To wait for the next Mission bus, can sometimes be twenty minutes (see Daly City 702.) I have a passenger who desires a location within one block of the Potrero gate. Such as by the KQED television station across from our yard, or in some other residence or business in nearby media gulch. All the hurry up and go home energy becomes a relaxed, enjoyable ride for one person I make special by dropping them off within a block of their destination. And the knowledge I saved them time without additional transfers instills that they are a part of a transit family within a great system. 'Unnecessary conversation' sometimes pays off. This goodwill can have expansive positive effects on the perception of drivers as a whole, and goes a long way to hopefully preventing calamities or funding arguments down the road.

Pulling In

ONE COMMON COMMENT PEOPLE MAKE when waiting for the bus is the question, "How come I see like three buses going in the opposite direction when I have been waiting 15 minutes for a bus and nothing is coming?" And this has to do with where the buses come from, and where they are headed when they pull-in. "Are you a 49?" is asked a lot when buses along Van Ness have the head sign reading, "Market." There is no line number displayed on the left of the head sign, just the words in bold, "Market." The truth is that this coach could be a 41 Union, a 30 Stockton, or a 49 City College pulling in to the wires on Eleventh Street and ending its run for the day.

Trolleys do not magically transport from their last terminal to the bus barn. They have to return to the barn on the wires, usually along a corridor that connects to the pull-in wires at various locations like 17th and South Van Ness, 16th Street and Bryant, Eleventh and Mission inbound, or 10th and Howard outbound. So when headway, the distance or time between buses, is gradually increasing after rush hour ends, knowing which direction the pull-in coaches are headed, helps, because service is superior in this direction. 49 line buses that go out of service inbound at Eleventh Street from Mission don't turn left on to Van Ness, and so the headway immediately increases for those waiting to go inbound to the Fisherman's Wharf area or North point. Someone waiting at a big corner like Van Ness and Market at 6 p.m., would see three times the number of buses headed outbound along Van Ness, because these buses are pulling-in.

The good news is, if you know the pull-in direction of buses heading back to the barn in the early evening, you get great service with buses almost empty and quiet. This is a great spot to find the Zen zone. Working a run with pull-in operators who do work is a great way to start a twilight shift with a gentle beginning. When operators do not pick up, or I am missing a leader, the load on Van Ness becomes an impatient, angry drag down.

When I pull-in from the 30 Stockton or 41 Union or the 49, I always try to pick up those waiting along Van Ness even though I am a short-line coach. Technically, based on the information on our paddles, our run's timetable, we are a 49 line coach. I have found if I pick everyone up, it helps the bus driver behind me going all the way to City College because he or she only has one major stop to pick everyone up: at Market. Sometimes I get permission to go down to 14th Street so that my passengers can connect easier with a 14 to continue outbound. It doesn't "cost" me anything in time to do this as a pull-in from 14th Street is actually sometimes faster than 11th, and it prevents a huge group of people from waiting at Market by Van Ness station.

There is nothing worse than having a huge group of people waiting for the next through bus and you are pulling in. By picking up folks willingly and taking them to a transfer point on Mission, it reduces delays for my follower and helps those waiting. Having a working PA mic makes my voice easy to hear and understand really pays off. This eliminates the battle cry from angry passengers on board when I turn off the line to go to the barn.

Sometimes, however, being mister politeness-man does not help. Anger remains unabated and no one understands how I am trying to help. In these cases, the right to remain silent is actually the best policy. If it has been one of those days, I have found it best to remain silent. Any thing I say can and will be used against me in a passenger service request. We have learned as operators that being helpful to stay in service to get folks closer to a transfer point, doesn't always work. More drama does not mean better service!

When I was new with a high cap number and low seniority, the probability was high the runs I found available in the afternoon had a pull-in at the end of the day. And if you have a lower cap number, and want to work days with big money, you may have to choose a day run split whereby you also have to pull in after a long twelve hour range during the day. The point is, after working for many hours, the last trip is a short line trip which involves taking the coach off the regular route and switching over to wires on streets which lead to the bus barn.

Interestingly enough, no matter how many years a San Franciscan has under their belt in living in the city, or riding a bus, if they don't have a friend or family member who has worked for or is working as a transit operator, they are clueless about what happens in the morning hours from 8:45 a.m. to 10:00 a.m. and around 6:15 p.m. to 8:00 p.m. Certain runs and certain buses end service during the end of a peak period of frequent service, to less buses and a longer headway.

Most people don't understand when peak period is, or that the headway between coaches changes every four hours, and is clearly marked at any shelter with a map. Most have confusion between express and limited service, and are unaware express service operates in only one direction depending on the time of day. Express coaches run inbound in the morning and outbound in the afternoon, and this of course, requires you know which side of the street you need to wait on to catch the bus in the correct direction of travel. And what lines go downtown, or which lines go crosstown and never see Market Street.

One intending for a coach headed in a direction towards the bus barn should look not at the line sign, but the destination as well. Especially during the times when headway changes. And after 14 years of service as a bus driver, the ratio or number of people looking at the destination sign of the bus has remained about the same. Less than one-in-ten standing on the sidewalk waiting for a bus, actually acknowledges the bus destination before boarding. And if the operator informs those boarding about the destination of the coach, patrons are confused or clueless about why the bus is a short line coach. Just as in the run from hell I worked in 2007, there seems to be an unlimited well of new, misinformed, or confused passengers about bus pull-ins after peak periods.

I guess if I could wave a magic wand of desire to change behaviors which chronically delay or add to tension between riding public and our union members, it would be this issue. It is simply a matter of awareness and pattern. And no matter how many years or how many hours at work we have been in the seat, the patience must be mustered to quickly and clearly explain that this bus is ending at 11th Street, or 30th Street, or Market, or 17th and Bryant.

Pulling Out

THERE ARE CERTAIN KEY POINTS around the system where operators begin and end their shift not at the bus barn. Eleventh and Mission is a relief point. It is a place where drivers take over the seat and relieve another operator per the run schedule. And at this corner, it is also where defective coaches can pull-in along Eleventh Street to Bryant and park the coach. Its also where buses from five lines pull-in from revenue service to the bus barn.

Because 11th and Mission is a pull-in / pull-out location and relief point, it is somewhat of a congregation point for bus drivers waiting to make relief. Coaches get new operators in staggered time slots, where successive buses on line get relieved. This occurs mid-morning around 10am. And later around 2 p.m. Knowing what peak periods are, when buses are entering and exiting the line, helps with understanding about why headway between buses increases and decreases. Most people don't seem to understand headway changes every four hours. There are also runs between those getting relieved so that if a bus arrives without a relief operator, hopefully, the driver who passes through without relief will stay in service. And these relief times, controlled by scheduling, can become a factor in spacing and wait time between buses. It can also cause gaps and overcrowding if there is not an operator or a coach to make relief.

One key point about relief points and pull-out wires is the awareness of where they are. Early morning commuters, and those trying to get home after a long day, would do well to understand where these key points are for the transit system in their city. When the time interval is decreasing between buses as morning peak begins, it pays to know where to stand.

Sometimes a few blocks makes a big difference in how long you have to wait. If you are getting off of BART at 24th Street and going outbound to Geneva and Mission or to a stop on the way to Daly City, then it pays (in time, and time is money), to know that just one outbound stop away at Cesar Chavez, all the morning pull-outs to Daly City, make their first stop after they turn off of 26th Street. Someone passing up the 49 at the 24th Street BART Station, is missing the chance to get on any number of 14 Daly City coaches pulling out and making their first stop at 26th and Chavez.

There sometimes is a shadow period of very few buses in the morning as owl coaches pull in, and fresh buses pull out. If you are aware of where these morning buses are coming from and where they enter the line, you can save yourself a lot of time in getting home or getting to work, if you know where to stand. The number of people waiting can also tell you how long it's been since the last bus passed. The average trolley wait can be determined by the number of people standing. Twelve people waiting means twelve minutes have passed. This is one of those cases where it pays to get on the "wrong" bus to transfer later on down the line. The important thing is to get past the pull-out wires on 26th, where plenty of empty buses are heading outbound to the Excelsior and Daly City.

If you want to go cross town on the 22 Fillmore and where waiting at Harrison inbound, you would find a nice empty 22 going your way. But if you were waiting at Potrero, you might end up being late, and become angry as you saw a 22 turning off route before your stop and going home to the bus barn. In this case just three blocks determine the difference between getting on a fresh empty bus, or seeing a bus turn off right before your stop. And this can have a big impression on how one views service. There is much knowledge about riding Muni, once understood, reduces the wait time to get somewhere and adds to being in the Zen as a rider.

Beach and Broderick

IF THERE WAS EVER A more tranquil and restful terminal on a busy line, it would be the peaceful residence location of the 30 Stockton terminal when I was working at the Presidio Barn a few years ago. Since I left the 30 Stockton Presidio Division line, the terminal has been moved to Divisadero and Chestnut, a location I thought was a better place. It has a switchback near here, on Francisco, and has a double track of wires for coaches to pass, unlike the single track at Beach and Broderick, which still is used on the head sign of the 30's out of Presidio, since it does more accurately describe the furthermost stop near a major tourist destination such as the Palace of Fine Arts.

So even though this missive may be somewhat outdated, the problem of headway and timing seem to still be a problem. And some of the problem about this terminal has nothing to do with the fault of management of the line, but in how we communicate with one another about need. And one of the important needs here is having a place to go to the bathroom, or water closet. Hot water, soap, and paper towels, are a precious commodity for a San Francisco transit operator.

Businesses, schools, or residences, and the people who run or live in the buildings close to our terminals have numerous fears about why there should be no bathroom for operators. And this seems to be related to the NIMBY symptom throughout our country. Not In My Back Yard, and I will go to any length to prevent a structure or permit for anything new or different near my house or school or business. And in seeing what the situation is like at other terminals, the fears of these neighbors seem unwarranted and selfish given the lack of problems around the placement of our other bathrooms. The sense of community and purpose for the common good has been lost in our society, and seems to parallel the rise of the car class as the means of travel.

Back in the streetcar days, we would travel together on transit lines that were more numerous and frequent. Most old timers alive today, and those of us who like trains, agree with a certain amount of fondness for the way things were. A lack of congestion on the roads is apparent in most old films and photos of this bygone era. Most would agree these simpler times held a higher quality of life. And some of the seniors who were young and alive then, are the most adamant about not placing a bathroom near their house. And this baffles me. Would you rather we urinate into cups and pour our tinkle in the gutter by your house? Do you think trash is diminished simply because there is no bathroom?

The old woman who would peer out of her house when our terminal was at Beach and Broderick, I was told was the main source of discontent for having a bathroom there. But doesn't the convenience of having a terminal outside your door count for something?

The return of the placement of the terminal back to Divisadero and Chestnut makes sense, but still NIMBY-ism is in full force with challenges to install a bathroom. No one seems to be transit oriented today. Those making the call to keep a bathroom for operators away, must not ride the bus and lack any sense of gratitude for why a carbon free mode of mass transit is better for the quality of our life. It is not that they are malicious, they just don't know.

Coach Trade and the Defect Card

As the buses warm up and get used, the dynamics change. What was once a great bus in the first four hours of service, becomes a creaky cantankerous old complainer. The back doors stop closing. The kneeler fails to rise. The brakes start to grab. Or the horn starts to blare without even touching the wheel. And so a chapter about the defect card.

In all my coach trades made, only once did the person I was relieving with my pull-in coach, fill out the defect card so I would know what to show the tower when I brought the coach in. Only once. Notice I did not use the pronoun operator, but the term, person. Because an operator is required to fill out the defect card. As fate would have it, on the one time I needed a defect card when I pulled-in, I did not have it. There is definitely a lesson behind this one. Apparently, my defect card slipped out of my paddle when I went to a coach at an alien division to pull out a motor coach. And this was at the same division where an inspector wrote me up for not having a time piece. This was the same inspector involved in the witching hour whereby I left the Ferry Plaza alone with a forty-five minute headway after a no power situation. Interestingly, I was the only coach with power to make it down to the terminal. And so, perhaps, may be a situation for payback was at hand. But if the RailwayGods have shown me anything, it is by doing the next right thing by working the rule, all is well, and the Zen zone protects.

I have to get over myself and not worry about what other people do. So when it comes to the defect card, if I can get a good idea about what is wrong with the coach, so be it. I can fill out the card myself.

I have found I get a better idea of what is wrong with a coach if I test drive, or rather, road test the coach myself. One common refrain from a "repeater" coach is when the equipment has a chance to cool down, most problems go away. I have withstood the test of time so that my body and experience can outlast the equipment. Not true for everyone. And if my physical body can outlast the equipment, then it stands to reason I must know the limits of the equipment and adjust.

One of the dilemmas I have is with the air. If a kneeler is weak, I have to determine which stops I can "get away" without using the kneeler. Most seniors reply with shock about why I am not getting the steps fixed, if the bus is not working. But they don't seem to understand by taking this bus out-of-service, the next coach will be even later, and without any seats at all. So, by staying in service and making due, no brownie points are forthcoming. Staying in service and making due just results in more complaints and no extra help.

So all I have left to do is to fill out the defect card and call on the radio if I have a safety significant defect. Wait for orders, and continue to march. There are no rewards (maybe on Maui) for an operator who tries to make due. I have been one of those operators, but this missive is causing me to realize this may have to change. But when I see a new operator having difficulty with their coach, I am reminded about how far I have come. Some operators like fast doors. Others like slow ones. It is not up to me to judge another's preferences. We all have our own style of driving. As soon as I give up my own defects of character, the easier the coach trade and pull-in. Amen.

Calling Central

ONE OF THE COMMON COMMENTS I get from operators, even those with time and with lots of experience, is the refrain, "I never call central." Or "Those guys are clueless." And I have found operators on the extra board fall into this category more than the average operator working a regular run on the same schedule every day. Extra board operators get to be assigned a new run on a daily basis. This is great when a sign-up drags on for months, and keeps monotony and boredom at a minimum, and it also prevents an attitude to develop from regular problems or passengers, because the operator is not on the same schedule day in and day out.

I believe some operators are "hiding out" on the extra board so as to reduce their accountability with the regular riding public. And this can be a very good reason. Especially when there aren't enough operators to cover all runs. But for me, I like the regularity to plan my time off by having a fixed schedule. Also, if there are recurring problems on my run and line, I get to take a look at what I am doing to cause these problems, and see if I can make them go away. That's why I like to do my "homework" during a sign-up and see if I can make a choice preventing headway problems or overload, though this is not always clear. Especially in not knowing who will sign on a low paying run as my leader.

"Central" is our shorthand for OCC: Operations Central Control. Even though nine of ten interactions with Central may not appear fruitful or necessary, it is the one in ten times when a call to Central, or from Central, is immensely helpful. And it is this one in ten that makes keeping a professional calm tone on the air really pay off.

The Dao of Doug

Central operators come to identify us not by run or coach number, but by our voice. And if they have come to recognize my voice and attitude as one of helpfulness or being brief and concise, all the better. One more tool to have at my disposal when I may need it. Yes, Central cannot necessarily see what is going on in and around my coach, so bearing this in mind, I don't get upset if they state something contradictory to what I know or can see.

A lot about what Central can see has changed recently. The new drive cams mounted on the front windscreen (windshield) has helped, as do the newer cameras in the newer coaches. Central Control is no longer in the dark about what is going on in front of our coach, and I believe this to be a good thing. Some would say this is an invasion of privacy, but I disagree because we are a civil servant in a job serving the public. Cameras are being installed around the common areas at our division for security purposes, and the drama queens are upset. If you are a public servant and carry yourself professionally throughout your day, what is the problem?

Yes, I do believe George Orwell is right: big brother is watching us in more and more places, but I try to keep this aspect on a positive note, hoping these images would capture an event that would protect me from abuse and falsehood. Much of the cost of litigation can be stopped dead in its tracks by the images captured on the coach. I look at the drive cam as my friend. So far so good.

I said that only one in ten calls may appear helpful, and these calls usually end in a tag line from Central we operators come to know all too well. Below are a list of the tag lines Central gives us, and the emotional component that goes along with them. These phrases may seem simple and innocent enough on this paper, in your armchair or desk as you read this, but believe me, when we get these directives, we are under a much higher level of stress or unusual headway.

"See the Inspector"

Usually occurs when things are very busy. Central Control may be having high call volume sometimes due to a major line delay such as when the tunnel gets blocked. We are silently expected to work an extra load without a break and we need a switchback for a mental break, or because we have been working for over two hours without a break. Sometimes, on a straight through run, we may have gone for four hours without a fifteen minute break. So we call for a switch back, usually ten minutes short of our final terminal. The answer from Central Control is to "see the inspector" for time and place. But nine times out of ten, there is no inspector! I usually pop the brake and wait and see. If no one comes to the door, I can call again, but this adds to the delay, and other coaches may be blocked behind me. "Take it to the end, and call back later." is the usual response. Not getting the break we need, when we need it, adds to the frustration.

"Take It to the End"

Usually a Central response after "See the Inspector." And even if we do make contact with the inspector, he or she says, "Take It to the End." Good is the day I can follow this instruction without a problem. If I am all alone, without a coach behind me, I follow this order, but if my follower catches up to me by the time I reach my last short route switchback, I call again. Many operators wise to this make sure they stay four minutes or more so the lead coach doesn't get a switchback. This makes for a long day unless we can turn it into a game, or our coach shuts down and we need a road call.

"Do The Best You Can"

When I cannot take on any more passengers because my bus is full, I call to let Central know I am beginning to pass up stops. This phrase comes into play when we are late and heavy. Many of our coaches have defects not safety significant, but are randomly occurring and cause delay, such as slow doors, and slow brake release. Fare box problems and lack of heat or air can also us to not feel we have been given what we need to do our job properly. Not being able to use the wheelchair lift or kneeler due to low air is just another curse to hear, "Do the Best You Can." But at some point, going out of service may soon become reality. This most frequently occurs when a bus is already missing in front of us. We are taking on more people, which adds to the bus performance issues, and adds to needing relief.

"Put It On the Defect Card and Continue in Service"

This usually pertains to a bad fare box or Clipper card service not working. But when a defect concerns our ability to pick up wheel chairs, a call is mandatory. Many times, the bus won't move if the lift does not stow. This is a bummer to have to clear the coach and tell everyone that the bus it out of service. So most times, of all the orders, this one is usually the fastest and easiest to follow. Hopefully, we can continue in service, but this is usually an order before another call to state we can't continue.

Things tend to go wrong in groups. Getting out of the bus to push the wheelchair lift to stow is one technique. Resetting master control and shutting off the bus sometimes makes the problem go away. Clicking on the traction control or rear door lock can make a problem go away, at least for awhile. This can make relief interesting. Because as a bus gets warm and stays in service, the performance starts to deteriorate. I am amazed at those who can make it to the relief point on time and not break down. So the lack of writing anything down on the card, and bringing it to the relief point, is an honor in and of itself, even though many take issue with this and feel the relief operator is not being honest. But given our own situation to end a part of our shift on time, bringing the coach to a relief point is better understood.

Breaking down and having to pull out may not be any easier than calling Central at the relief point, and calling the shop. So the decision to stay in service is up to us and not Central, and the order to continue in service lends itself to conflict with others: passengers and coworkers alike.

"Help is On the Way"

Make sure you have something to drink or eat in your bag. Make sure you have your reading glasses or reading material also. As any professional driver can attest, you never know when your shift will end, or how long you will have to wait in the dark or cold wind, for a road crew to assist you in getting back on the road. We are required to call back at regular intervals to check and see when help will actually arrive.

There are some good times and some bad times to ask for help, especially during a shift change. Faced with the prospect of waiting in the cold, we do try to keep going as best we can, without delay. But many times this is impossible because the bus will not move. "Help Is On the Way" can have our eyes rolling because it seems like a bad joke. We operators can balance this equation when we get asked the question, "Is there another bus behind you? "Yes," we say, as we close the doors. Thank God you never said "when." And even when it is asked with the phrase, "just right behind you?" since we were never given any units of measure, such as in blocks or in minutes, the answer, "yes," is still an honest one!

But lest we forget, we never know who is listening, so it is best to remain calm and stay professional. Doing so has given me the switchback or pull-in I really need to go home just at the right time. Answering incorrectly can put me under the microscope for other problems, and this usually does not end well in the superintendent's office.

"See the Dispatcher"

It's like go see the boss. You are in trouble, and have to go to the Principal's office. Perhaps this is the most insidious message from Central because of the ambiguity. What could possibly be the reason I need to see the dispatcher? Is it an off the cuff, oh-by-the-way, afterthought in a message, or a stand alone call. It's effect for bewilderment and despair is best used alone. Do I have mail? Did the man waving his cane at me as I passed him up call 3-1-1? Did the guy in the wheelchair who blocked my bus, completely full, on Van Ness at Market have a friend in the MTA office? Did the woman who said she knew the Mayor personally, as she repeated my cap number under her breath as she stepped off, really actually know the Mayor? Was that sarcastic comment by the lead dispatcher this morning a tip off they knew what was coming? I must be employee of the Year! (hah) These and a thousand other thoughts roll around in our heads as we try to guess why Central, in their busy day, thought it necessary to call us about seeing the Dispatcher. Maybe it is a drug test. What would happen if I just happened to forget as I trudged up the steps after pulling-in? In any event, I can't remember any good reason for when I had to see the Dispatcher. Which begs the question, is it better to pick up mail at the end of the day or right before a pull-out in the morning? After work may be the winning answer.

And now I see I be lying, because there was the time I received two commendations in one day! And today they actually let me go home from my doctor's appointment, instead of having to return back to get my letter signed! So like any 'good' operator, I embellish the story with pain and suffering to gain sympathy, and hope this will change the outcome of discipline to a favorable decision. It never does. The decisions are usually made in advance. It's kind of like the Cardassian system of justice. Guilty until proven innocent.

But when a passenger comes forward with a phone number and a line of support, it all seems to melt away. Which reminds me to say it is always a good idea to have a courtesy card in our jacket pocket. These are cards which a passenger can fill out as a reference to an unusual occurrence on the bus. Usually a phone number is enough. We (should) keep them with us, so all you have to do is ask. When someone observes I am doing a good job, and goes out of their way to let me know, the Zen zone returns, and the rest of the trip is uneventful.

Shoes

"BABY NEEDS A NEW PAIR of shoes." That's what I say when I am hitting hard, or I see sparks at night off of my collectors. Shoes are the carbon blocks sitting inside the brasserie or metal brackets that form a slot at the end of our trolley poles. This is the point at which we collect our power from the overhead. The shoes sit inside of the collectors. 600 volts of direct current are fed through the feeder wires which come from certain utility poles which carry the wires upon which we travel.

Next time you are on a hill by some trolley line, look for the poles which are carrying the power. You can see the wires coming directly out of the pole and on to the overhead. If too many buses are too close together, especially on a steep hill, the power breaker will go off and we will temporarily lose power because the feeder wire cannot handle the load. This shut-off of power, or a tripping of the circuit breaker can occur leaving Chinatown on Sacramento Street heading outbound up the hill to Nob Hill, and also on Union Street leaving Van Ness inbound. It didn't take me long to learn this fact.

Heading inbound on the 41 Line, I was not too far behind two smaller coaches that started across Van Ness as I pulled into the zone to pick up a few runners. But because the next stop at Polk is on a steep hill with a short green light, the two buses did not clear the Polk Street stop as I crossed Van Ness and began to climb. Sure enough, as I got close to Polk, they started to move on to Larkin. But this is one of the steepest grades in the system. Since no one was waiting at Polk, I did not kill the light, but proceeded ahead before the light turned red. I figured the other buses would be on to the next block before I crossed Larkin, just as business as usual such as in the Mission line I was familiar with. Big mistake. My pull on the power caused the bus in front of me to slow down dramatically, and I put the pedal to the medal, but the bus came to a stop. I looked back and saw another bus crossing Van Ness and beginning to climb. There were now four buses in three blocks, loaded with passengers getting to work, and two of us were stopped.

I put on the parking brake and waited for the bus in front of me to start moving. Fortunately, he was able to start moving forward once I stopped draining energy from the wires. But another bus behind me was starting to climb from Van Ness, and sure enough, I saw the bus in front start to slow down as the bus behind me started to hit the steep grade. I won' t follow too close from now on. The feeling of powerlessness when I put my foot down on the power pedal, and start to lose power on a hill, with a full bus, is not something I would like to experience again.

Having a traction brush fail is also another scary movie. In departing Chinatown for Nob Hill, I lost all forward traction on the bus. And the parking brake would not hold the coach, either. All I could do is hold my foot on the service brake, and call for help. One thing I did forget about was when the air in lines reaches a certain point below 60 pounds per square inch, the emergency brake will pop up and hold the coach. But this is a small comfort when the air in the lines is not holding the coach at a higher pressure. Did I really want to test the pop–up and see if it would hold? Luckily, it did. But I sure hope I never get that coach again when I am leaving Chinatown during peak period!

After rain for a week, all the carbon dust built-up on the wires gets washed away. This is great for keeping our hands clean, should we need to use the ropes to replace our poles on the wires. But not good for wear and tear on the carbon shoe. It cuts faster into the wire because there is no more dust to act as a lubricant. The groove in our shoe gets deep. Our collectors hit the hangars and crossovers with a loud ka-chunk, and our poles drop down off of the wires. We need new shoes.

There is a special slot in the range of the poles where we can hold the pole down to look at the shoes. This is at about a 45 degree angle from where the pole attaches on to the roof of the bus. We can look to see if the carbon is cracked or deeply grooved. Sometimes when we look there is no carbon at all in the collector! We cannot drive the bus forward from that point and must not move until the shop arrives and replaces the carbon. And when we have new carbons, we still have to be careful in crossing other wires, because the slot in the new carbon is very small, and the poles can fall off of the wires easily.

Now, the shop checks every coaches' carbons when we pull in after a.m. rush. They also check the temperature to see if our shunts are working and we have enough swivel. This helps keep the Zen!

Paying attention to how hard the coach is hitting the wires is good for staying in the Zen of driving a bus in San Francisco.

Wheel Blocks

"Unbelievable, just unbelievable." This is the statement of a resident nearby the La Playa bus terminal by the Ocean Beach Safeway. It was recorded for the Jon Stewart Show. This was a comedy show, and the occasion for the recording was based on the fact that this man's garage was hit by motor coaches more than once. Motor coaches rolled away from the terminal and ran-in to his house. Not once, not twice, but three times. On the video, he replays the incident of how he fell out of his chair when the bus hit. Hilarious for a television show, not so funny for the operator of the bus, and in training class. Our training department shows this video to make a point about the importance of using a wheel block to prevent an unattended coach from rolling away.

Ocean Beach is not the only place where motor coaches rolled on the loose. Daly City, at the end of the 14 line, buses have also caused much damage to buildings and cars. The front wheels can roll over the curb and run into parked cars, or if the wheel is not curbed, can roll all the way down the hill and into a building at the first intersection after the pull-out from the terminal. One may wonder how this could happen. Inattention to detail is usually the first line on a disciplinary letter we receive when we are in trouble. There really is no excuse. I sometimes forget to use the parking brake when I am in the yard which is flat, when I am in a rush. If I am adjusting a mirror on track four, I sometimes only open the doors instead of setting the brake. But whenever the seat is vacated, the brake must be set. I can only imagine what could cause an operator to forget to set the brake. Perhaps there was a distraction from someone asking a question, or the rush to get to the bathroom. In any event, it is hard to justify any reason why the brake is not set. I have not found anyone who could agree this could be excused.

When I was out with an inspector being re-qualified (Requal) we came to the outbound terminal on the one line at 33rd and Geary. Requal occurs after we have a chargeable accident. We have to be graded and evaluated by a training inspector to make sure we are doing everything correct to insure safety. But every now and then, it is not the operator on the training coach who gets into trouble. Sometimes, a blatant error is found by another operator on another coach. Case in point. Out at 33rd and Geary at the One Cali lines.

A coach was all the way back in the zone, and had not moved up as other coaches had moved up. I could not clear the cross walk on the turn before the terminal, so the inspector grading me asked to be let out and to move the unattended bus up to the lead space in the zone. The door was closed, so he put his hand in the drivers's window to open the door from the door dial. As soon as he pushed it, the bus released the air brake and started to roll back into my coach!

In one sweaty moment, the instructor was able to collect himself and rush to the open driver's window and stop the coach by opening the front door using the door dial. The bus stopped within two feet of my bumper. After overcoming the initial shock, we waited for the operator to return. Although words were said, no write up occurred.

I later found out disciplinary action was taken, and I saw the operator one last time before he went in to the superintendent's office for his hearing. I never saw him again. There is no excuse for not wheel blocking the coach, or for not using the parking brake. He had about ten years with the company at that time.

With good eyesight and hearing, it doesn't matter how old you are to start working as a driver with any company. One important fact not too many people understand about driving jobs is that age discrimination is virtually non-existent. Because the testing of blood pressure, vision and hearing are mandatory for licensing, and demand is high, driving jobs are always available. But inattention or complacency can rear it's ugly head at any moment, and with it comes the loss of the job.

RDO

REGULAR DAY OFF. IF A workweek goes by and I have kept my sanity, I can test my body and mind and see if I can work on my day off, my RDO. If I haven't turned crazy by working my run during the week, I can see if I can "get away" with making extra money on a day off at the overtime rate of pay. I know if I have mastered the Zen of Muni if I can work my regular run, and still have the energy to try more work, if it is available, to get ahead of bills, or save for a vacation or toy. One of several things can happen. If I have had a good week, a few hours of work on the weekend can take the Zen vibe away real fast if I am working an intense line without a leader. The good news is folks who would have to wait twice as long to get picked up, have the service they expect, because operators work on their day off.

The best thing about RDO is going home after the day is done. Just made bank at 41 dollars per, and it's over! Uncle Sam takes away half, but if a holiday is involved, payday is a breeze. The law of diminishing returns does make itself apparent on payday, though. And I have seen that if overtime hours exceed 26 per pay period, the amount of fatigue or hangover from working on a day off, becomes not worth the extra hours due to taxes. Working three days of overtime in a two week period takes such a toll on personal time, I am no fun to be around on or off the bus. I have to be careful I don't get a PSR, Passenger Service Request. PSR's result in mail. We find our paddle missing in the receiver's office before we pull out, and we have to go see the Dispatcher and sign off for our mail.

Trying to explain our life to our loved ones at home, our roommates, or anyone who tries to reach us by phone is a chore. We are not sitting at a desk in an office. Our schedule can change at any time with traffic, construction, fires, parades, protests and equipment failure. If you have a jealous lover or in a home situation without trust, then this job may not be for you. Sorry, got to go! I have to move my bus up because my follower needs room at the terminal. I have only 3 minutes to take a bite, can I call you back later? I am sorry my phone is off, I am not allowed to have it on!

I now try to say, I gotta go, or I won't be able to call you back for an hour. Voicemail is great for leaving a message, but don't expect us to be on the line if you call right back: we are already on the road! Most of my friends now know what to expect when it comes to unavailability on the phone, but it does take some getting used to. Sometimes months. Sometimes years. We can't just call whenever we like. The schedule is just a guideline, really! Kind of like the Pirates Code on *Pirates of the Caribbean*! But just as Captain Jack Sparrow, we too have to make it up as we go. So if you do have an Operator on your address book, know this: we never know what is going to happen next. If you wonder why we aren't arriving at the arranged-for time, hey, we took Muni!

Keeping it Zen adds that sixth sense, the intuition that helps our loved ones and friends understand, dinner may get cold before we get home!

The Zen Zone

THE BEST TIME TO WORK Muni is when the bus has an empty aisle and half the seats are open. This occurs in the morning on most major holidays and on Sunday mornings. The aisle is empty and half the seats are empty. The pulse and rhythm, the ebb and flow of passengers is steady state and harmony abounds. During the week midday, usually from 10 a.m. to 2 p.m., with leader in sight, is also a wonderful time. Good job, good pay, and no threats on the horizon. It is the wish and hope of every transit operator to select a run where the Zen time is maximized. Everyone is relaxed and happy and the schedule flows perfectly. Every time I do my homework before a signup I try to find this zone in a run, and try to guess where this zone is, and how it can be sustained for four or more hours per day.

And it is truly a complex matrix. One false move, one error in judgement can be a costly mistake resulting in trips to the superintendent's office, and love letters from the dispatcher. A love letter is at best, a piece of mail containing a caution and re-instruct, or if close to the danger zone, a warning in boldface, which means, you are off the hook for disciplinary action, but if this happens again within a short time frame, your goose is cooked. The goose being time off without pay. Imagine coming to work in the morning and the first thing you see is that your paddle is missing from the row. Go see the dispatcher, you've got mail. What happened this time?

Everyone asks me what the bad lines are. And my answer is that none of the lines are bad. On another day, I might answer all the lines are bad. Timing is everything. Which is true for a stand up comic, a worker on an assembly line, and as a waiter or cook in a restaurant. So here is what most riders don't understand: its not what line you are driving, but when.

For example, do I really want to be leaving Clay and Drumm on the 1 California line at 5:02 p.m., as Embarcadero Three's elevators are filling up to capacity, dropping hundreds of workers to the city streets to pick up a bus to go home? Or should I be at the other end of the line at 33rd Ave and Geary, hours after school has let out, to be headed inbound in non-peak direction, only to arrive downtown an hour after most people have gone home? Do I want to be the first 22 Fillmore leaving after the bell at the Marina middle school, where hundreds of hyped-up middle schoolers with more hormones than they know what to do with, after hours of being cooped up in school, be knocking on my door as I try to pull away from the inbound terminal at Bay and Fillmore? Or would it be better to be leaving Third and Twentieth in Dogpatch, around 3 p.m., hours before all the blue collar workers around Potrero Hill start clocking out? And so it isn't what, but when which makes or breaks a good run choice.

And I think something could be said about applying this principle to our daily work and our job. Are we usually not so bothered about what we have been assigned to do, or are we really upset or angry over *when* the task is expected to be completed? Sure, we can try to work late, and I have seen the glazed over look on your faces when you board the bus at 6:30 p.m., or, perhaps follow this suggestion. Try getting your boss to change your arrival time. Fat chance.

There is a pecking order I have discovered in and when people go to work. Early is better. At least when judging by faces I see boarding the bus. First, we have the humble Latino working class off to fisherman's wharf. The bus boys, the dishwashers, the true working class backbone of the city. Then we have drones. The white "middle class" working stiffs who work downtown for something, something and something, whether it be an architectural firm, or a law firm, or an advertising agency. I see the fresh young up and comers first. They are going places and have probably moved here from somewhere else for their first big break in the big city. They have the smile behind their eyes which is full of promise of a great new job with a resume that probably says I am new and trainable and not bogged down from a dysfunctionally drugged family past from having grown up in California. They say, in their eyes, I got away from my one horse town with the single blinker light.

Then come those who have been here awhile. What, forgot to shave this morning? Painted the town last night? Tie one on did you? Or they come rushing out of a doorway without their tie on, to finish the windsor once they get on in the aisle, now crowded, as the inbound arriving time approaches nine o'clock. And after the clock strikes nine come the mid-level managers. Lattes in hand they head for the corner office. Those in echelons whom eschew the time clock for a supervisor role or particular grade or rank in an organization downtown. And the school trip. Youngsters much quieter in the morning than in the afternoon. Quietly and purposefully podded-in to their music, or contemplating their day ahead.

And then the moms and their babies. Off to the daycare, or to do the daily tasks of running a family. And then come the ancient ones.

The seniors off to some food shopping or their appointment to see the doctor. And then, the Zen. The midday time when everyone is at work or at lunch. And this is when rush hour is over, and when most morning runs pull-in. Where we transit operators can lay down to chat in the Gilley room, or go to the gym to work out. Maybe its a trip to the post office, or the store. For those lucky enough to live in the city, we can go home to do chores. But for those straight through runs, this is the Zen time, when things are steady and even, and usually not full of much drama.

And so I have a word of wisdom to impart. Try coming in early for a week. Don't tell anybody. See how on time and smoothly Muni runs at 7:30 a.m. versus 8:30 a.m. You can always clock in at the regular time: but this time you've already made it up the elevator. You have time to get coffee. You are within seconds of the time clock, not minutes. You could actually wait to punch in right on the dot. And guess what, your trip-in was a few minutes shorter, maybe as much as twenty minutes shorter if you didn't see buses passing you up, stacked to the brim.

If I had any magic wand to wave, it would be to stagger start times in half-hour intervals so that not everyone had to be at the same place at the same time. You'd be amazed at how much work you can get done before everyone else traipses in. So if you think its not a good idea to ask your boss for a different start time, try it anyway and see what happens. By lunchtime, I'll bet you'd have everything done you were planning to get done, anyway. There is so much down time after lunch anyway, you may find a few nice surprises along the way.

So, staying in the Zen zone is the sweet spot that makes living in a big city with a good job with good pay a wonder to behold, with everything right in the world. But heaven forbid the run in front of you happens to be an open run with no regular operator. Or a run that has days off of Tuesday Wednesday, that usually doesn't get filled on a regular basis. This hit or miss wild card, not knowing who is ahead of you, or whether or not you have a leader, creates possible destruction of the Zen zone. Should I adjust up or down in my running time? Will I be running hot if my leader cuts in late with a last minute detail from dispatch? Did I piss off the dispatcher the other day by questioning how they do their job? Am in a payback situation? Payback is a bitch, a phrase or term I will never forget. Especially when Central Control has me on ignore, or the inspector at the checkpoint won't even look at me as I pass. And this is when the Zen zone can become Muni's ninth level of hell.

There are nine levels of hell at Muni, which, now that I think about it, should be at least another Chapter in this handbook, but suffice it to say here, one should leave the ninth level of hell after one trip, because the ability to sustain the ninth level of hell is very limited, and though there are heroic epics of being able to sustain this for four trips a day for over two weeks at time, eventually, the dam will break. And become the damn. The valley of the damned.

I will never forget the signup from hell. With no end in sight. But I was warned by a member of the executive board that this was to be a long signup. I remember making my choices for my choice slip before the signup at the Presidio. And my hero, my union rep., was standing right beside me as I saw the run with big pay and weekends off, still available on the range sheets minutes before my choice slip bid window. Wow, I said, here is a big run with weekends off still available. How could this be?

There are times when the runs pick us, rather than us picking them. Interesting, I thought, this must be a sign from the Muni gods I had arrived in my seniority level. I finally was able to get a 300 dollar plus run with weekends off during a good time frame, between 7 a.m. and 7 p.m., with some standby time for lunch. Little did I know, there was a reason why the run was still open. It was the icon for the ninth level of hell. It did the 1 line from 33rd Ave and Geary leaving just after 8 a.m., with an arrival downtown just after 9 a.m. And it passed the avenues just after the last express downtown. Which meant panicked office workers, who just missed the last express, would ask me at the door if another express was coming. No problem, I can do this. After a couple of weeks, they would realize that by 8:22 a.m., if they hadn't gone out their door, they would miss the express. It would just be a small matter of weeks, and the questions would stop.

But they never did. Week after week, different workers would be late, and a bad dream turned into a nightmare. But little did I know, two other factors were at hand to add icing to the cake from hell. My leader and follower were out to make my life miserable, whether by intention or design, I set in motion trains of circumstances I thought I didn't deserve, but were ripe for the picking. And so I believe this is a natural progression to move on to the next chapters, 'Witching Hour' and 'The Ninth Level of Hell.' . .

Witching Hour

Perhaps in five minutes after 5 p.m. when all the elevators fill with office workers ready to go home. Perhaps it is senior citizens looking out their window and seeing the rain has stopped and the sun is out. Perhaps it is the classroom bell ringing at Marina Middle School, signaling the end of the school day. Or the end of a baseball game, a Niners game, or the last fireworks grand finale. All these things have a different time of day or night, but would fall under the phrase, "witching hour." And this hour is the time, just like out of *Mad* magazines' panorama cartoon collage, with everyone from every part of the city saying the same thing at once, "Let's go before the mob starts!"

Would you really like being on a run that leaves the Ferry Plaza at 5:05 p.m., especially if there are tunnel problems? Or would you rather be in Daly City leaving in the non-peak direction, with a few baby sitters or house cleaners returning home?

Would you rather be leaving the industrial area near dog patch on the 22 after 5 p.m., or in the Marina, a residential area, hours after school has let out?

Does your run leave Fillmore and Bay five minutes after the bell rings at the largest middle school in the system, or would you already be on the road ten minutes away from the school, heading up the hill past Union? At Muni, just like in stand-up comedy, timing is key.

Leaving time from the terminal never had more importance. And many times we never know exactly when the clock has struck, or the shot was fired. All we know, with a sinking feeling as our bus fills up before we even get to the second transfer point along our run, that we a going to get "beat up" on this trip and get killed. Oh and by the way: Crazy can show up at any time, any place!

But lest we forget the skip stop rule, and when our bus gets loaded to capacity, we no longer have room, and can't take on any new passengers. The fault, dear Brutus, is how the hell do we do it and avoid the ninth level of Muni hell!

The Ninth Level of Hell

WHENEVER I FIND MYSELF IN the ninth level of hell behind the wheel of a large automobile, in my case, a trolley of Muni, I try to ask myself how did I get in such a place? And it is by an essay such as this that I can backtrack to find my part in how I got there, and to hopefully avoid ever having to experience this again. Without having to put on my favorite *Talking Heads* album. Hell, even getting to type this page was at least the seventh level of hell, and I wasn't even driving a bus!

Just getting a change in my default printer on my net book took forty minutes. Endless tries to not get my first printer off of default, and to check wireless connectivity took most of the first fifteen minutes. The damn first-note program refused me to change to my second printer, and once there, I ran out of black ink, and the old cartridges would not fit as the number 56 is bigger and has more ink than the damn new ones numbered 60, which have less ink, yet cost the same. I clicked to the company website to see about selecting a new cartridge and got it all in German, from a German website.

And whoever thought getting a new wireless router to share printers on a LAN should be sent to Guantanamo without a key or visa. Even with the USB cable plugged-in directly, one still cannot get the printer out of its dumb printer stopped mode. And then opening the mail program to send my rich text files in my windows starter net book, did actually work seamlessly and so fast, I was pleased to see this aces the mail application on my macbook pro.

But of course all my emails downloaded to my net book and I couldn't stop the avalanche of viagra and cash prizes I had won in my spam filled cue. Finally, after deleting all the emails off of my emailing program on my net book, I shut down the computer, which wouldn't close for new updates (lord knows what they were,) and on to my macbook, where low and behold, my email was there with my first four rich text chapters of this book. And after a few stuck-on-stupid spinning wheels that would not download, I got all my .rtf files converted to pages, and could print them on my first printer which still has black ink. Yes! Total time elapsed: 1 hour 20 minutes. Geez.

Final Solution. Go to preferences cue and search apple for Software Updates.

Needless to say I have my issues. And driving the bus seems easy compared to my office travails. I am looking over this previous paragraph of vomit, and seeing my tranquility has been disturbed. Just as it does when I am behind the wheel of a large automobile, or in my case, a bus. But my spiritual research has indicated that I have the freedom of choice in how I be with respect to what is going on around me. I may not be able to think my way out of the ninth level of hell, but I can choose at any time, how I feel. And when I can't get into the Zen zone, I had better take a deep breath and reboot.

The fare box was jamming up and I needed to keep resetting it. Passengers were complaining about being pushed and shoved. I was without help in front or behind, and no buses were in sight. I was losing it. I made a decision. I can't stay in this mind set. The 18th Street switch was right in front of me. I clicked right on to 18th, and left Mission. "This coach is Out Of Service" "Awww." came the response from the packed bus. Unauthorized Pull-In. I opened all doors and people slowly streamed off the bus. Not without some comments about my abilities or my mother! This was the only time I recall I defied procedure and went out of service without permission. At this time I lacked the ability to control my load and check in with myself about my mental state.

Fortunately, I had another senior operator on board and she told me what I needed to do, and what to say to the dispatcher when I went to ask for another coach. She had boarded and was returning to the barn to pick up her car. Her day was over. I had forgotten about this ninth level of hell, and how she may have saved me from suspension or dismissal. She recently reminded me of this event. Wow. In my own self centered-ness, I had conveniently blanked it out. But I am glad I recalled this when I looked at how I had veered from topic. Interesting how I am in denial about all of this.

So, I guess all I can say in conclusion is that we all get into our own ninth level of hell, and can only hope and pray we have an angel around to help us when we can't do it alone. Thanks to the operator that happened to be on board riding, for helping me reach 18 years with the railway, and for keeping me employed through the years!

Daly City 702

ONE OF THE TOOLS ALWAYS at the disposal of an operator is the 702. This is the three digit 700 code of numbers that describes certain incidents over the radio to Central Control. And the code number 702 means the operator is taking a twenty minute break as a comfort stop to use the rest room, or, to collect oneself after a shaky security incident or some such event or events after a heavy stressful trip. And this is made clear in training, that the schedule is not important, and if you need a break, a 702 is always allowed, primarily because this is a necessity for safety: To keep the driver sane and safe as recovery time at a terminal may not be enough.

And perhaps there are operators out there that know when and how to use a 702 effectively. I do remember one time on the 24 line when I used a 702 and it seemed to send an effective message to the temporary inspector at 30th and Mission that I was not going to run to the end of the line because I had been late all day, and my switch at Cortland and Hilton was refused. I felt elated I had done the right thing and the break was well deserved. But this is the only time in 18 years I can remember taking a 702, and taking it because I was denied a switch.

There were many more times I could have done this, and may be my accident record or disciplinary record would have been cleaner if I had taken this option that is always open to me. But my desire to stay in service usually always wins over, and I seem to doubt that the fine line between staying in service and taking a break is spread evenly throughout the system. Or that operators use this as a necessity instead of a privilege, and whether or not this right is abused. Because we hear of talk in the Gilley room of those that are constantly taking 702's, and the havoc it can wreak on their follower. How would one define that which is abuse, and how could one stop it or determine any discipline should be meted?

And this intellectual exercise always ends in futility. Because it is the emotional feedback in the present that is the key. What other's think, and trying to adhere to the schedule is my drawback to blocks of receiving. And being present in the moment about the near misses or angst from passengers, should be the key to take a brake, and take a break. Only when I start getting thank you's from passengers do I know I am back on the right path.

When I am neutral about my leader taking a break, and not worrying about the outcome, can I clearly see whatever passenger load I may have to take, all will be well, if my attitude is not one of being put upon, but of being of service. I then begin to build compassion for the other operator doing what they need to do to stay safe. If I try to compare their actions with my own needs, I fail. If I take a step back, and focus on doing the next right thing, the pain of taking on a double load goes away, and I find those I pick up are grateful for my handling of a heavy load. So I have realized it is not how hard I am working, or how late I am, but how I am feeling inside, and where my focus is. By not allowing myself into victim mode, all is well, and a 702 from my leader is inconsequential to how I view my day. Actually, when I am doing well in a busy day, I see the number of people I pick up has little to do with my success.

But the Daly City 702 seems to be the ultimate challenge to letting things go. An operator friend of mine was describing the Daly City horror of his two leaders both going on break at Daly City, the outbound terminal of the 14 Mission, a straight shot from the county line to the heart of downtown with the terminal at the Ferry Plaza. He had a pull-in from Daly City, and was in a small coach. When two 60 foot coaches would go out of service, he had not enough room to take all those who were waiting. And they would become angry when his full coach would pull up to the stop with a short line destination of 30th Street: half-way to downtown, and short of the first major BART station.

And all of the tools we are supposed to take to cover ourself failed. I too had been in this position one the 1 California, and the 30 Stockton. Not enough time or room to take in all who were waiting. And if this was a one time thing, no biggie. Tomorrow is another day. But when his two leaders were going out of service day after day at the end of his busy shift, just as my leader was passing up on a daily basis, staying neutral becomes next to impossible.

Calling Central Control for a switchback to avoid Daly City was denied. Talks with the yard starter for a bigger coach would only yield a larger coach for a day or two. Miscellaneous reports filed after work could backfire as being labelled a snitch. Complaining about the God given right to a break holds no water. The only apparent thing left is to take the matter into our own hands, and let the cards fall where they may. And this means putting up Garage, or going out of service without authorization. In a way, if no inspector seems interested in doing anything about the problem, then hey, what the hey, I can get away with pulling in out of service. And many operators do go out of service on their pull-ins, and cause a heavier load for the next coach following behind. The hope is that retribution, or what goes around comes around will come full circle, but the time frame of payback seems remote and unfair in the here and now.

I took switches unauthorized at Folsom, to make relief on time, and sarcastically went on the air about it, and it took three years from the day, to finally make amends to the street inspector who heard my sarcastic call about taking switches on my own. What was I thinking? I wasn't. I was angry. I could not seem to get his attention at Union and Columbus, the midpoint of my last trip. But in hindsight I should have popped the brake and talked to him direct. My thinking had already been off, because I refused to go to end of the line and see how late I actually would be at relief. This is my downfall. I take matters in to my own mind without waiting to see if my relief is really that angry with me being late. As it was I was making relief early. I never really gave going to the end of the line an honest shot. And I was placing too much thought on what my relief thought of me or how "bad" it would look if I was late. I was so concerned about what this senior man thought of me that I sacrificed my duties and responsibilities on my own last trip.

So my friend did what we do. He put up 'Garage' and picked up no one. He switched back early at Lowell. He picked up what he could, and then became express, not stopping to pick up the small pockets of folks at the intermediate, smaller stops. And to try to stay out of trouble, mix it up so it is impossible for anyone monitoring to make conclusions about what we are doing wrong. But all this has the exact opposite effect. The attention comes to us and what we are doing wrong, and not on the operators that are causing the problem. This got me in hot water, and is where discipline falls on the person trying to make the best of a bad situation, and not the true cause. The saving grace that has kept me employed is I must divorce myself of what other's are doing, and just operate the best I know how. And I have learned the hard way in the beginning, not to make bold statements about others, or boast about what I am doing to others. I never have had a good social skill to discern my enemies from my friends. But when I do get honest, the answer always comes. I never talked to anyone, and I never got the answer. But I do now.

Payback only comes in the form of the next sign-up. And if a sign-up from hell continues, oh well. The length and duration of pain can be meted out in the long run, and I have to look at it this way, or else I am doomed to discipline I think I don't deserve.

So I always talk directly to my follower and leader, and never let it go beyond that. When I find out why they do what they do, I take it in stride and feel confident I have done all I can do. And this has led me to the Zen of driving an electric bus.

Payback

THEY SAY ITS A BITCH, and it really is. Problem is, half the time I never knew I was receiving payback. I was having a bad day without knowing I was the cause. And it took me years to see the cause and effect my actions of pissing off others had when this energy boomeranged back on me.

The first most obvious payback was one on one with other operators. That's when an operator waits the full time at the terminal, and then, after waiting past my leaving time, goes out of service. By the time they call Operations it is too late. The damage has been done. I have double headway and am leaving late. The clincher is when I have no follower so I can't rely on help from behind. And the worse place for payback is at Bay and Fillmore. No way can the three major stops of Chestnut, Lombard, and Union be passed up, and no way can I enjoy an empty or light segment of load before the mid way point on the trip. Oh well. There goes the Marina Green Middle School's Out bell! Better luck next time.

Or the famous Daly City 702. Where two twilight operators, usually junior to the pull-in coach behind them, take a twenty minute break so that the pull-in operator has a long headway to pick up passengers from Evergreen, Lowell and Geneva all the way into the inner Mission. Instead of shadowing behind two in-service coaches, the operator has to pick up an extra load for the three miles into the pull in wires. And not just for one day, but over and over, day after day.

And when passengers retaliate, it is usually up front and obvious. They pull your poles to disable your forward power traction motor.

Or they release the air from the rear door, so that your interlock engages, and you can't move the bus forward at all. May be they stand in front of your bus. Perhaps they park their wheelchair in the street. Or throw their bag into the side of your bus. In any event, you are not going anywhere. And I can mark my progress as an operator when this stops happening to me, even at classic corners like 16th and Mission. I am happy to say by being in the Zen zone, I have not been blockaded by passengers for years.

If you want to make a difference about service, don't expect immediate results. If more than one person calls in a complaint, odds are better. Getting the time and place correct counts: are you inbound or outbound? And the coach number is usually adequate. But the operator's descriptions can be humorous. I was once called a Latino male. I was thrilled. I didn't even care about the complaint. I was glad to be thought of as from spanish or mediterranean dissent. Hair styles and glasses also seem to add to the humor. Sometimes this is the best part when reading the complaint.

But heaven help the operator under the microscope of management, lying in wait for a minor mistake, as if there aren't enough things to worry about, already. In using the full set of rules to the exact letter of the law, it is only a matter of time before the suspension comes. Opening a door early, or squeezing a lemon out of a stale green, odds are you are going to get written up for not following the rules. But, by swallowing my pride, not taking things personally, and looking at all my actions to change my behavior, once the penalty is received and not disputed, I have been given a new chance to avoid the penalty box. I am born again with a clean slate, and can make sure I don't keep repeating the same mistake over again. I look for feedback from my passengers. If I keep hearing thank you's when people step off, I know I am on the Zen track.

When Worlds Collide

It wasn't until I looked through my old journals that I finally found an answer I had been looking for about why I was on the black list of an important street operations inspector who has dogged me for many years. And I have been replaying in my mind, what I could have done differently to have saved the job of an inspector that was volunteering his time for the good of the order during a power failure along the Mission line.

There had been a power failure on Mission somewhere probably due to wires down, or a short or heat sensor going off and tripping the breaker to turn off power to the wires along Mission near downtown where Mission parallels Market Street, and perhaps to about 25th Street in the heart of the Mission. I had made it to the inbound terminal at Ferry Plaza and waited for 45 minutes until power was restored. I was amazed at the sense of humor I had as I told the inspector this trip was going to be one for the history books. No coaches in front of me from downtown to Van Ness, and all I had was a small coach. And little did I know what was in store for me at the 11th Street stop near Van Ness. I was packed, stacked and racked, and was ready to pass up the large crowd waiting at the stop. I had no intention of stopping to pick anyone up because I was completely full from picking up all stops from downtown.

And to my horror, I saw an inspector herding like a shepherd, seniors off of the curb towards my bus in the traffic lane. I had intentionally stayed away from the zone to pass up those waiting, but was stopped in traffic waiting for the light. Big mistake. I have since never got caught waiting for a light after a pass up. I learned early on where and when not to get in a stall if a pass up was necessary.

So here were passengers being guided towards my front door with no room at the inn.

"I can't take any more people, this coach is full," I said to the inspector. "Make room. Ask people to get off to make room for these seniors." And a mutinous roar went up in the bus, "Hell, no." "Make them wait." I shut the door and moved ahead with traffic that was flowing after the light went green. I better cover my self on this one. I pushed the button to call Operations Central Control. After run, line, and direction, I asked the question, "Is this coach full?" I held the mouthpiece up to the aisle. "Yes!" responded the entire group crammed in the bus." Whew. I had an alibi. As long as the passengers were on my side, I knew I would be okay and not get into trouble. But I definitely want to stay out of controversy, and obey my general orders.★

★the views herein may not reflect those of the SFMTA or its employees.

Reprise

MAKE NO MISTAKE, I DO sing on the bus. And although I am a bass clef brass baritone player, I consider my younger brother as the musician in the family. I'll claim the writer title as I have an English degree from the University of Missouri - Columbia. Completing my degree became a challenge as I became increasingly angry and frustrated at failing to see how the memorization of stale facts was important or necessary to thrive as a young adult in the job market.

When I slammed the door shut on the Dean of Arts and Science because I failed the Romance Language requirement for graduation,

I didn't realize that the taking of Spanish conversation was the only practical class I would later use as a bus driver in the Mission district in San Francisco! The Dean's door glass remained intact after I left the office. It was the classic institutional wooden door with his name hand painted in black on the glass panel inset. Just as in a roadrunner cartoon with Willie E. Coyote, there was a delay in reaction; it later shattered into a matter of pieces not unlike the shards seen in a damaged bus shelter, or curbside from an auto break-in overnight. *Walking on Broken Glass*, by Annie Lenox seems to be a reprise in the music of my life as a transit operator in San Francisco.

Another possible label to this missive would be the title of a book of a writer employed at UMC when I was in the creative writing sequence in 1980 and '81. I had the pleasure of being in Thom McAfee's writing class. Thom was the published author of a book with a title that seems to typify the life of a transit operator in any major city in the U.S. or the world, for that matter. The title of Thom's book: *Whatever Isn't Glory.*

And so it goes. My vice-principal, so to speak, associate superintendent at my bus barn, politely asked me to wait for the right turn red light at a brand new terminal loop by City College at the Phelan Loop off of Ocean Ave. I wondered why he was sent to this terminal and why he asked me to wait for a green. Little did I know that the next day, everyone in upper management would be watching on a screen at Central Control via my new drive-cam mounted on the front windscreen.

The next day, I pulled away from the terminal as usual when the coast was clear: not a car in sight and no student pedestrians coming from classes; without waiting for the light to turn green. The sensor in the ground did not adjust the countdown in any measurable way, and, like the newly painted lane markers, was completely useless in functionality. In my mind, the engineers had failed again. The electric trolleys should have been given the two right tracks, the diesel number 8's the longer space on the left track. The 8 had more recovery time than the trolleys and hence needed more room. Why anyone put an arrow in the red light was beyond me.

I had heard later from a friend in engineering, and a worker at the loop that it was a mistake to not get input from the drivers about redoing the terminal. So I was to be the whipping boy to demonstrate how we operator's were to use the right turn: go when the way was clear, and to ignore the signal.

Beep. Beep. My radio went off after I made the right turn on my first red arrow. *Did you see that you went through a red light?* I was distracted by answering a passenger's question and should have just used this as an excuse. Instead I argued with Central's unnecessary intrusion. Big mistake. This was the frame for book 2, Keeping Zen, under scrutiny until a suspension could be issued. It wasn't until about I was halfway through writing Dao 2 that I realized what had happened. I should have just kept my mouth shut and agreed with Central Control.

Later that same day, on my lunch break downtown, a senior in a wheel chair was right behind the leading wall in Powell station, ready to push himself in front of an outbound train. I immediately wheeled him away from the edge of the platform and asked for help from the station agent. But in leaving to get help, he jumped off of his chair in front of an M Oceanview. Luckily, he was out of his chair and was far enough away from the front wall such that the operator of the M had just enough time to slow and stop. Because the senior was out of his chair, he landed conveniently between the two rails, and was not seriously injured. Here is the dramatic extreme of discipline on the first day of a new lane configuration, and a rescue of an attempted suicide in the underground.

But the happy ending to this violation was a year later when I did the 49 trolley on my day off and got ready to leave the Phelan Loop terminal. Yes, this time I planned to wait for the light to turn green!

But when I looked up at the overhead signal, and instead of a red arrow, I saw a solid red light! They had changed the red arrow to a solid so it was legal to make a right on red! I was floored! Victory! I don't care if this sounds selfish: I'll take it! This was an unsung heroic action in which I played a part for change. I felt the bigger victory in the solid red than pulling away the man on the platform!

So rather than being a hero, I was set up to face the music, so to speak. I understand that not needing help from above or below is not the same as having a use for an angel or light worker of this universe. As Neale Donald Walsch points out in *Happier Than God* not needing God is not the same as having any use for God. As God has said, and shall always say, *I am always with you, even unto the end of time.*

That the end of time may be short at the end of the line, does not mean I should try to 'make time' by pushing a stale green, or moving before a red turns green! The biggest demon I face is believing that I do not have enough time. And that demon is me!

Glossary

paddle: our timetable or schedule that we pick up in the receiver's office that comes with our defect card and books of transfers. This entire bundle is called **an outfit.**

pre-op: usually done on a track in the bus barn and is a term for checking mirrors, lights, radio, horn, doors, wheelchair lift, kneeler, bike rack, collectors, poles, retrievers, operator chair and the set up of the fare box. Operators are given 15 minutes to ready a coach for revenue service.

pull-out: pre-op-ing a coach on a track at the bus barn to prepare the coach for revenue service. Denoted on a run schedule by a star ★ These coaches cut-in on a line somewhere on the middle of a line.

pull-in: going home. Coaches are taken out of revenue service, somewhere in the middle of the line. Example: 14 Mission line coaches pull-in at 11th Street, usually outbound and on 25th Street inbound. Coaches on the 49 line pull-in at Market outbound, or 25th Street inbound. 49 line coaches may also pull-in on 11th Street, 14th Street or even 18th Street.

leader: the run and coach in front of you

follower: the run and coach behind you

leader's leader: the run and coach two buses ahead of you

follower's follower: the run and coach two headways behind you

not-out: a run not scheduled to pull out, usually a four hour period on your run of schedule

pole-dropper: a coach whose bushings are stiff and locked in an unfavorable position, usually when a coach makes a right turn, so that the poles drop off the overhead wires.

slack brakes: a coach with an abrupt braking transition to the dynamic braking at 3 m.p.h. from the air brakes

hill holder: a toggle switch which holds the coach on a hill without the necessity of applying the service brake.

master: the on/off switch that also has a park charge setting for recharging the coach overnight

service or courtesy lights: the lights that come on when the doors are open. The green light over the rear doors means it is safe to step down to activate the rear doors.

run sign: the three digit number in the lower left of the curbside windscreen, denoting what run number is assigned to the coach and operator at the time the coach is in or out of service.

road call: maintenance assistance from the shop to service a vehicle and bring it back into revenue service.

sick on the run: going out of service in the middle of an operator's scheduled run

daily detail: a posting of all runs not held by the usual operator

rdo: regular day off

ci: classified industrial: operator out on leave due to illness or injury on the job

hol: operator's day off due to legal holiday

move up: given by street operations by street inspector or operations central control, and gives permission to leave early from terminal.

pre-empt: a tripper mechanism located in a small box in the wires, favoring a green for an oncoming coach.

far side: not a gary larson cartoon, but a bus zone after crossing an intersection

nearside: a bus zone located before an intersection.

bus bulb: a bus zone mid-block where the sidewalk is moved out from the curb lane.

flag stop: made without the bus coming to the curb, usually because another vehicle is in the zone, or a regular bus stop made by or between parked cars. Example: 17th and Kansas is a flag stop both inbound and outbound on the 22 Fillmore.

coach stop: any location where a yellow marker indicates the line number of where you can pick up a coach by signaling for a stop.

multiple line stop: a bus stop serviced by more than one line. Always a good idea to indicate to the operator before approach to the stop that you want to board the coach indicated on the head sign. looking away is a sign you want another line coach.

head sign: the line and destination of an approaching coach located on the front, sides, and rear of the coach.

destination sign: next to the line sign indicating the coaches' final stop. Always good to be mindful of short line pull-in coaches having a different destination as peak period ends, usually from 5:45 p.m. to 7:45 p.m.

line sign: the first sign on the head sign which shows you the line number of a coach. If blank, yellow, or red, usually means that coach is short line and pulling-in somewhere in the middle of the line. New coaches display, "Ask Driver."

transfer: issued after fare is paid, good for ninety minutes to board another coach to reach your destination. Note: all lines finish one trip in about 45 minutes, so the time given allows you to go to the end of the line and still have time to catch another coach to get to your destination.

headway: the time in minutes between coaches, and changes every four hours.

transfer point: a place where two or more lines cross or meet.

inbound: a bus headed downtown or to fisherman's wharf. Jackson and Fillmore, Aquatic Park, Pier 39, and Fort Mason are considered inbound destinations.

outbound: a bus headed away from downtown, or from fisherman's wharf. The Avenues, Dog patch, Potrero, and Third Street are considered outbound destinations.

peak period: that four hour headway between 6 a.m. and 10 a.m. in the morning, and 4 p.m. to 8 p.m. in the evening. Many coaches go out of service in the middle of the line before 8 p.m., which creates the illusion more buses are going in one direction than the other.

streetcar: any number of cars that run on rails and can be the new Breda Light Rail Vehicles, Milan Historic streetcar, or PCC

trolley: an electric bus with rubber tires that has evolved from the box-like vehicle that used to run on rails.

articulated trolley: commonly referred to as a double bus, these electric buses are sixty feet in length and have a joint between the front and rear section.

getting the swerve on: shaving every second of every minute to move up after being delayed, such as by a slow leader.

Muni: short for San Francisco Municipal Railway

Zen zone: that joyful and meditative space on the bus when all is calm